Courage has Wings

Courage has Wings

Betty Greene

Irene Howat

CF4·K

10 9 8 7 6 5 4 3 2 1

Copyright © 2017 Irene Howat

Paperback ISBN: 978-1-5271-0008-4

epub ISBN: 978-1-5271-0048-0

mobi ISBN: 978-1-5271-0049-7

Published by Christian Focus Publications,
Geanies House, Fearn, Tain, Ross-shire,
IV20 1TW, Scotland, U.K.
www.christianfocus.com;
email: info@christianfocus.com

Cover design by Daniel van Straaten
Cover illustration by Jeff Anderson
Printed and bound by Nørhaven, Denmark

Contents

For Magnus Iain Harris,
my grandson

Wreckage

The waves on Lake Washington lapped over Betty's feet.

'Now, don't you go paddling in the water,' said Joe. 'At least, not till I go in with you.'

Betty didn't in the least mind not paddling for there was so much to see. Her brother Joe was hauling part of the fuselage of a small aircraft from the lake. She could hear him puffing and panting with the weight of it. After he landed it on the beach, Joe swam further out and brought back another piece of wreckage.

'What's that?' four-year-old Betty asked.

'It's another bit of the aircraft,' he explained, as he shook himself like a dog when he came out of the water. 'Come and I'll show you.'

The girl jumped up and ran to her brother. He was eight years older than her and seemed so grown up.

'Look, see!' said Joe. 'These are parts of an amphibious aircraft that crashed into the lake.'

'What's a fabulous aircraft?' asked his little sister.

Joe ruffled her hair. 'It's not a fabulous aircraft,' he grinned. 'It's an amphibious aircraft.'

'What's that?' Betty wanted to know.

'Come and I'll show you as well as tell you because I've collected quite a bit of it now.'

As they walked along the lakeside Joe explained, 'An amphibious aircraft can take off and land on water. This one crashed when it was coming in to land.'

'Was the pilot hurt?'

'No,' Joe told her. 'He bailed out on time.'

'I hope he could swim,' the little girl said.

'I'm sure he could,' answered her brother. 'I don't think anyone would fly an aircraft that takes off and lands on water unless he could swim. Now, come and see this.'

Joe pointed to each piece of wreckage and told Betty what it was.

'This is part of a float,' he said. 'The floats keep the aircraft from sinking. And there's the cockpit where the pilot sits.'

'Can I sit on the pilot's seat?' asked the child.

'I don't think so,' laughed Joe. 'I've just hauled it out of the lake and it's waterlogged. I think Mum might not want you to go back home soaking wet.'

'Look! There's something else in the water,' yelled Betty.

'I think it's part of the aircraft's wing,' Joe told her, squinting against the evening sun to see what he could see. 'You have a look at the bits here while I swim out for it. And please don't fall and hurt yourself. I don't want to take a wounded sister home.'

Joe walked into the lake until he was nearly out of his depth before starting to swim. And it wasn't long before he appeared back, dragging part of a wing behind him.

'What have you two been up to?' Dad asked, when they arrived home much later than usual.

'Joe pulled a fabulous aircraft out of the lake,' Betty told her dad and Bill, her twin brother.

Dad laughed. 'That would be the amphibious aircraft that came down,' he said. 'We'll go tomorrow and have a look at the pieces.'

'May I go?' asked Bill.

'I'll take you,' Betty told him. It was a good feeling to have seen something exciting that her twin hadn't seen.

That was Betty Greene's first encounter with an aircraft. But that was fair enough because it was 1924 and there weren't all that many others around then.

Joe was very keen on aircraft and took flying lessons when he was fourteen years old.

'Do you want to watch Joe's lesson?' Mum asked one day.

'Yes, please!' the twins said in unison.

They climbed into their car and Mum drove them to Renton Field, a landing strip not far from their home in Medina, on the shores of Lake Washington.

'That's a single-engine Curtiss Oriole,' Betty told Bill, as Joe sat at the aircraft's controls and the engine roared to life.

Her twin was much more interested in cars than in aircraft. They watched as their brother flew the small aircraft round Renton and eventually back to the airfield. He even managed to land with only a few bumps along the ground. Joe must have been good at what he was doing because he was flying solo when he was still fourteen years old!

Betty admired her older brother so much that for a long time she thought he was the best pilot in the world. That was until 1927 when a very wonderful thing happened and made Joe fairly jump up and down with excitement.

'Charles Lindberg is coming to Seattle!' he said. 'Please, please can we go to see him?'

Mr and Mrs Greene grinned. 'I think we'd all like to see him,' said their mum.

Charles Lindberg was a real hero. He had just won the Orteig Prize for flying solo and non-stop from New York's Long Island to Paris. That flight made him the first person in history to be in America one day and in Europe the next.

'How long did his flight take?' Betty wanted to know. She was as fascinated by aircraft as Joe was.

'It took thirty-three-and-a-half hours,' said Bill. 'The flight was 3,600 miles (5,794 kilometres) long. That means he flew at an average speed of 107 miles (172 kilometres) an hour.'

Bill was good at maths!

The family went to the stadium at the University of Washington to see Charles Lindberg fly overhead in the very same aircraft that had crossed the Atlantic Ocean.

'It's called *Spirit of St Louis*,' Joe told Bill, though his little brother already knew that.

Captain Lindberg circled round the stadium and then flew off. Betty felt somehow let down. She would have loved to have seen the pilot who had done such a wonderful thing.

'Charles Lindberg's coming back,' Joe said, knowing exactly how she felt for he felt exactly the same. 'He's going to land at Sand Point Naval Air Station and come back at the head of a motorcade.'

The mention of a motorcade made Bill's eyes light up. He loved motor cars, and the bigger and more powerful they were the more he loved them.

A short while later there was a cheer from the far end of the stadium. Dad lifted Bill on to his shoulders and Joe lifted Betty.

'Do you see them coming?' Mum asked.

They could!

Suddenly the whole stadium was filled with noise.

'Lindberg! Lindberg! Lindberg!' people shouted until they had no voices left.

That night, safely tucked up in bed, seven-year-old Betty thought she could still hear the voices shouting out the pilot's name. And, when her dad came in to kiss her goodnight, she turned over in bed and said sleepily, 'Lindberg.'

There were four children in the Greene family. Joe was the oldest, then Al. After that came the twins, Bill and Betty. All four went to church and Sunday school every week with their parents. In fact, it was their dad and mum who started the Sunday school in Medina. It wasn't just what they were taught on Sundays that showed the Greene children how much the Lord Jesus meant to their parents, it was also how they saw them living day by day. This was especially true one day in May 1928.

The twins were having a great time at a friend's birthday party about quarter of a mile from their home. They had played some games and it was time to eat the birthday cake.

'Come and sit at the table,' said the birthday child's mum, as she pressed eight candles into the cake.

There was a scramble of hungry children and then silence as they watched the candles' flames flickering. The birthday child took a deep breath and blew all of them out.

'Happy birthday to you! Happy birthday to you!' the others all sang and then the cake was cut.

'Would you like a piece?' asked Mrs Greene, who was helping to serve the children.

Bill and Betty grinned. Would they like a piece of cake? Of course they would!

Just then the phone rang. It was for Mrs Greene, who looked puzzled as she spoke on the phone. Then she looked worried and turned her face away from the children.

'A fire?' she said, keeping her voice low. 'Our house is on fire?'

Putting down the phone, she rushed to the door. Opening it, she looked along the road and saw smoke. The Greenes' house was ablaze!

All the children were taken back into the party and Mrs Greene was rushed up the road by car. By the time she arrived at her home the fire was well ablaze. Knowing that Betty and Bill would be very upset, someone ran down the road to tell them that nobody had been hurt, that everyone was all right. The twins tried very hard to join in the party games but they couldn't concentrate on them at all.

Some hours later, when the fire had been put out and there was no chance of anyone being harmed, Betty and Bill, along with their brothers, dad and mum walked round what had been their home.

'There's nothing left,' said Al. 'Nothing at all.'

But Betty could see something she recognised. 'There's a piece of my doll's china tea set,' she whispered, pointing to a little bit of broken saucer. 'And there are just handles left from my chest of drawers.'

Joe looked around at the remains of their home.

'The only things that haven't been burned are the two garden chairs that were on the back porch. 'Someone must have moved them away from the fire,' he told his little sister.

The family all stood in silence looking at the blackened wood and the strange shapes all around them.

'We've so much to thank God for,' said Mr Greene. 'No-one was hurt. Everyone is absolutely fine. We've only lost things and things don't hurt when they go on fire.'

Betty thought about her favourite doll and was sad, even though it wouldn't have felt anything when it burned. Then she thought about her brothers and her mum and dad and was truly glad that not one of them was hurt.

There was a little wooden house in the grounds of the Greenes' home and they moved in there.

'The rooms are tiny,' said Bill. 'And there are hardly any of them.'

Mrs Greene smiled. 'What you mean is that our home was big and the rooms were spacious. There are many, many families who have to live in smaller houses than this one.'

Betty thought that the cottage was a bit like a doll's house and decided to enjoy living there.

Just at that moment there was a knock at the door. It was the mum from the party home.

'I've brought down some clothes for the twins,' she said, handing Mrs Greene a bag. 'And some towels too.'

'And I have some saucepans and dishes,' added a friend, who arrived a minute later.

Then there was another knock. This time the gift was clothes for Al and Joe. And as Mrs Greene closed the door she noticed that someone had left two bags of food on the step.

'People are so kind,' she said, as the family opened up all they'd been given. 'Look, someone has even remembered that our Bibles were burned in the fire.'

Dad took the Bible from Mum's hands, opened it and read some verses to the family.

'Let's pray,' he said, and they all closed their eyes.

Dad thanked God for keeping them all safe and for their kind friends who had given them the things they needed.

That night the twins whispered to each other before going to sleep.

'The fire was exciting!' Bill said quietly. 'At least, it was exciting until I knew it was our home.'

Betty wasn't sure if she agreed. Fire somehow seemed a bit too dangerous to be exciting. But nobody was hurt, she thought, as she fell fast asleep. And

God, who had looked after the family when their house went on fire, looked after them in their new little home.

Excitement in the Air

When Bill and Betty were in sixth grade their teacher liked reading stories to her pupils as much as her pupils enjoyed listening to them. Sometimes the story was about World War I and the air fights above Europe. The twins talked about these stories all the way home from school.

'The Vickers FB5 was the first specially designed fighter aircraft,' Bill said, as they walked. 'And it was better than anything Germany had at the time.'

'Not for long though,' Betty pointed out. 'The German Fokker E1 was much better. Its synchronised gear meant that gunners could fire through the ark of the propeller without hitting the blades.'

'Shooting your own aircraft's propellers was never a good idea,' her twin said. 'I think that Max Immelmann was the best pilot. What do you think?'

'I think that's what I want to be,' announced Betty. 'If I could choose to be anything in the world, I'd be a crack pilot ... but not in a war. I'd like to be a peacetime crack pilot.'

Bill looked rather puzzled. 'I'm not sure that we need crack pilots in peacetime,' he thought aloud.

The years that followed were exciting in the world of aviation.

'Look at this!' yelled Betty, waving the daily newspaper in the air. 'Amelia Earhart has become the first woman to fly across the Atlantic Ocean.' Then she read the article more carefully. 'Oh, she flew as a passenger, not the pilot.'

Even that was very daring at the time and more was to come. Amelia Earhart did several long solo flights in the United States. For a while she was Betty's hero.

The following year there was more interesting news.

'Do you think he'll make it?' Bill asked his sister.

They were talking about Richard Byrd who set out to fly over the South Pole. A base camp named Little America was constructed on the Ross Ice Shelf and expeditions by snowshoe, dog-sled, snow mobile and aircraft began. On 28th November, 1929, Richard Byrd and three others flew their Ford Trimotor to the South Pole and back in 18 hours and 41 minutes.

Betty thought about aircraft, talked about aircraft and even dreamed about aircraft.

* * *

'What would you like for your sixteenth birthdays?' Mr Greene asked the twins, in 1936. 'You can have a long think about it and let us know.'

Betty didn't even need a short think about it. She knew exactly what she wanted – a flight in an aircraft! As that's what Bill decided too the pair of them had their first flights aged sixteen years exactly.

Bill and Betty could hardly believe it when they opened their birthday gift from their uncle. Each had been given $100! They had never seen so much money! Their uncle probably thought that they would use the money when they went off to college, and that's exactly what Bill decided to do.

Betty thought differently.

'Dad and Mum,' she said one day, as the family ate a meal together. 'Would you mind if I spent my birthday money on flying lessons?'

Mr and Mrs Greene thought about it and talked it over with their daughter.

'All right,' they decided. 'As long as you keep enough of the money to buy some clothes, you can spend the rest on flying lessons.'

Betty grabbed them both and gave them such a hug that their ribs probably ached!

Not many days later Betty met her instructor. His name was Elliot Merrill.

'Jump aboard,' Mr Merrill told her, and watch every single thing I do. Don't just look at the view. You're here to learn to fly not to admire the scenery.'

He didn't really need to say that for his new pupil wanted to fly more than she could put into words.

'This is the rudder,' he said, pointing down to his feet. 'That's what decides our direction. 'And here's how you set the wing-flaps for take-off.'

Betty watched carefully. 'Is that where you set them for landing too?' she asked.

Merrill smiled. That's what he liked, a pupil who asked sensible questions!

'I can't believe that you've done your first solo flight,' a friend laughed, just two weeks later. 'Is it not seriously scary?'

'No,' grinned Betty. 'It's seriously exciting.'

The sixteen-year-old would love to have studied for her pilot's license, but her birthday money ran out before she got that far.

'You'll have to save up for more flying time,' Elliot Merrill told her.

His pupil looked sad which was not at all like her.

'It will take me a very long time to save up enough,' she said. 'The last job I had was picking cherries and that didn't pay very well.'

'Were you allowed to eat as many cherries as you liked?' her instructor asked.

Betty grinned. 'Yes,' she admitted, 'and I still love cherries!'

The time had come for the twins to do some thinking about what they were going to do with their lives. Bill decided to go to the University of Washington to study mining engineering. The university was close enough to home for him to travel every day. Betty just couldn't make up her mind.

'I would like you to study nursing,' her mother said. 'You could do a degree at the University of Washington and then you and Bill would still be together.'

Because they were twins that had an appeal for Betty, but her heart wasn't in nursing at all.

'Nursing is a good career,' encouraged Mrs Greene. 'You can travel the world as a nurse.'

When Betty thought of travelling the world it was as a pilot, not a nurse. But she signed up for the course her mother chose for her and was probably the least enthusiastic student in the whole of Seattle.

It was 1937 and the twins were first year university students. Bill was happy and his sister was not.

All of her first year at university was a struggle for Betty although she really enjoyed the journey each morning and it was certainly unusual.

'You don't exactly live next door, do you?' a student friend asked, when she heard how the twins travelled.

Betty grinned. 'No,' she agreed. 'When we hear the whistle on the ferry, we head out and either run or walk down to the dock, depending on how sleepy we are. The ferry journey is amazing; a 2 mile (3.2 kilometre) trip on Lake Washington is the perfect way to start the day.'

'I think I might agree with you,' her friend laughed. 'What I wouldn't like is your long walk from the ferry to the university. I'd feel I'd done a day's work by the time I arrived and would be ready to go home.'

Laughing at her lazy friend, Betty was honest enough to admit that they didn't always walk the whole way, though they often did.

While travelling to and from university was a pleasure to Betty, being there was not.

'Mum and Dad,' she began, at the fireside one evening, 'I am SO unhappy.'

Her parents knew what was coming and waited to see what she had to say.

'I'm just not made to be a nurse,' she admitted, tears gathering in her eyes. 'I know nursing is a great thing to do. I know nursing would give me a good job. But … but, I'm just not the kind of person who is happy nursing. And I don't think that an unhappy nurse would be a good nurse.'

Eventually Mr and Mrs Greene agreed that, if Betty was still unhappy at the end of her second year at university, they would allow her to drop out. When the next session ended they didn't even need to ask how she felt. When she walked out the door of the nursing class for the last time Betty was happier than she had been for months.

'It's all very well knowing what you don't want to do,' her dad said, 'but what do you want to do?'

That was a big question and one for which Betty didn't have an answer. However, there were some things about which she was quite sure. Taking a pencil she wrote down her thoughts.

I'm a Christian and I want to serve the Lord Jesus.

I LOVE flying.

I love working in the church and doing any kind of mission work.

I really like animals. Maybe I could work with animals.

I like music.

I like people, but I really, really don't like nursing them in hospital.

After thinking about it and praying for God to show her what she should do, Betty spent a year working in her father's office, studying music and helping with her church youth group in Seattle.

One day the young woman decided to visit someone. Many of her friends were about her own age, but this one – her name was Mrs Bowman – was about fifty years older than Betty! Sometimes older people, especially older Christians, are a real help when you want to think things through.

Over cups of coffee they talked about this and that. Mrs Bowman realised that something was troubling her visitor but she didn't push her to say what it was. She sipped her coffee slowly and waited patiently. After a while, and some more coffee, Betty began to explain her problem.

'I just don't know what to do with my life,' she said sadly. 'But I feel I should be doing more than working in Dad's office.'

Mrs Bowman didn't rush her answer. Eventually she said, 'What do you really love doing?'

Without any hesitation Betty told her friend that she loved flying and she loved mission work.

Mrs Bowman smiled. 'You know, it seems to me that God often makes us love doing things so that we will do them. That's sometimes how he shows us what he wants us to do with our lives. For example, some young women just adore children and God leads them to become teachers.'

Betty listened to what was being said and let it sink deep into her brain.

'You mean that God might have made me love flying and love missionary work so that I could be a missionary and somehow use flying as part of my work?'

Mrs Bowman looked thoughtful. 'Is that so impossible?' she asked.

'I don't think there's a flying missionary in the whole wide world!' smiled Betty. 'But that doesn't mean that there couldn't be, does it?'

She was thinking aloud rather than asking a question.

Her friend was a wise woman and didn't push Betty's thinking at all. She let God do the moving and she let her visitor do some dreaming!

Imagine how Betty Greene felt at the very idea of spending her working life doing both mission work and flying. The more Betty thought about it, the more right it seemed. As she wanted to serve God above anything else, she prayed about it and asked him to make it possible, IF that was what he wanted her to do.

Once again the family was eating a meal when Betty had some news to share with them.

'There's a civilian pilot training course being run at the University of Washington,' she said. 'Do you think I could apply for it?'

Because she had dropped out of her nursing degree, Betty would have understood if her parents had said 'no' right away. They didn't. In fact, they actually encouraged her to find out more about it.

This was in 1940 and people were becoming more and more interested in flight because World War II was raging in Europe. America was not, at that time, involved in the war but pilots were being trained just in case they were needed. None of the trainees were women. It would never have crossed anyone's mind that a woman could fly a fighter aircraft!

Women Airforce
Service Pilots

It didn't take Betty long to discover that the course was open to women and that she had better get her application in quickly as the places were filling up.

'We can take a maximum of forty students,' she was told.

Of the forty eager students who met in their lecture room on the first day of term, only three were women.

'I don't know why they're here,' one of the male students grumbled. 'All the places on the course should be kept for men who could serve in the military if the U.S. joins in the war in Europe.'

Betty and the other young women were used to such comments and discovered that, if they ignored them, they could even impress their fellow students by their flying skills. At the end of the course Betty was awarded her Private Pilot's License, which also covered piloting aircraft with floats. There was a definite advantage in attending a university on the shores of Lake Washington!

* * *

Mr and Mrs Greene were away from home when they met Mrs Ethel Sheehy. They could hardly wait to tell their daughter about her.

'Mrs Sheehy works with WASP,' Betty's dad told her.

'WASP!' she gasped. 'Did you tell her about me?'

WASP was the Women Airforce Service Pilots. Betty had read about them in the newspaper. The organisation was formed so that women could serve the military. They couldn't serve as members of the military forces, but they could help by doing things that airmen usually did, thus giving the men time to do other duties.

'Mrs Sheehy told us a bit about the work of the WASP,' Dad said. 'They do things like move aircraft from the factories where they are built to where they are going to be stationed. It sounds interesting work.'

'It sure does!' agreed Betty. 'Did you get Mrs Sheehy's address?'

Mr Greene handed his daughter a piece of paper.

'I thought you'd want to contact her,' he grinned.

In next to no time Betty went to meet Mrs Sheehy.

'Your parents told me that you already have your Private Pilot's License, and for float-planes too. That's very good,' the woman said. 'You are certainly eligible to join the WASP.'

'Could I do that right away?' Betty wanted to know.

'Y…e…s,' Mrs Sheehy admitted slowly. 'But from what I understand your father and mother think you should finish your degree at university first.'

Betty was disappointed. 'I know,' she agreed. 'But I wondered if I might join the WASP instead.'

Mrs Sheehy looked at Betty's eager face but shook her head. 'I agree with them. You should finish university before you join us.'

Betty Greene did go back to university and she studied how people in different cultures live. She chose that subject because she knew it would be interesting. God led her to choose it because he had special plans for her future that would involve working alongside people from very different cultures.

A surprise was in store for Betty Greene. She discovered that if male students were going into the military, the university gave them their degree ahead of time. What did she do? She asked if she could get her degree in order to join the WASP and the university agreed.

'I don't know how you do it!' her twin brother Bill laughed aloud. 'You are just determined to get up in the air as soon as you possibly can!'

Bill too joined the military.

Betty became a member of the WASP and was told to report to Sweetwater, Texas. She could hardly hold in her excitement as she travelled.

Courage has Wings

On the first day at Sweetwater the new recruits had to appear in class, and it was a fashion parade like no other. All the young women were dressed in regulation olive green 'zoot suits'.

'I can't believe my eyes,' thought Betty, as she looked along the line. Two or three recruits in front of her there was one young woman who was less than average height. 'She can hardly walk!' Betty thought, and didn't know whether to laugh at the funny side of it or cry for the poor new recruit's embarrassment.

The legs of the girl's zoot suit were so long that when she rolled them up around her ankles the rolls were so thick that she was quite unable to walk and had to waddle along like a duck. Not only that, but the crotch of the suit was hanging down below her knees threatening to trip her up at every step. There was giggling all around but by then the funny side of it had gone from Betty's mind and she just felt heart-sorry for her fellow recruit.

'Excuse me,' she said, after they'd finished class and she'd caught up with the poor girl. 'How about we swap zoot suits? I think they've given you the biggest one of all. If we swap over, this one will fit you a little better.'

The girl grinned. 'Thanks so much,' she said. 'I was in danger of falling flat on my face and I thought I might be kicked out of the WASP and sent home if I did that on day one.'

Another girl who overhead what was said joined the pair of them.

'I think we were all in such a stage of giggles we were more likely to be sent off home than ever you were.'

Betty, who was (5 foot 10 inches) 178 centimetres tall was still drowned in the swapped-over zoot suit, but not quite as drowned as her new friend had been!

That night the WASP recruits were more like a sewing group than pilots. Nobody seemed to have a uniform that fitted. All were cutting off the ends of legs and sleeves and then hemming them up to make them fit. The small girl whom Betty had befriended had most to do. She virtually cut her uniform apart and made it again. Even tall Betty had to lop a bit off the legs of her one before it really fitted.

By the time Betty joined the WASP the United States was fighting in World War II. Of course, that was a great encouragement to Britain and the other Allied Forces. Now the female recruits were really needed to free up airmen to fly in battle. That didn't mean that all the men made them welcome, some certainly did not.

Before many days had passed their commanding officer spoke to the new recruits.

'Look on either side of you,' he barked.

Betty and her new friends looked down the line of recruits to the left and to the right, wondering what they were meant to be seeing.

'Only one out of every three of you will make it to graduation,' he informed them.

That wasn't exactly encouraging but it made Betty determined to be one of those who passed.

The first aircraft they flew were Fairchild PT-19s. There were two cockpit seats, one behind the other. A recruit sat in the front seat and her instructor sat behind her. Both wore earphones so that they could communicate with one another above the noise of the aircraft's engine. Because the Fairchild PT-19 had an open cockpit the engine noise was very loud.

One day Betty was waiting in the line to fly when a plane landed and taxied to a halt. She could hardly believe her eyes. The instructor was safely strapped in the back pilot seat but the front one was empty! The only thing to show that there had been a pilot when the aircraft took off was a set of earphones dangling over the side. The horrified recruits just stood and stared. Their friend, who was piloting the aircraft, either hadn't fastened her safety belt properly or it had failed during a spin sending her hurtling towards the ground. Thankfully she thought quickly and pulled the rip cord on her parachute. Instead of plummeting to the ground and certain death, her parachute opened and she descended slowly and landed safely. From that day on none of the WASP recruits had to be reminded to check their safety belts.

* * *

Betty's instructor was a bit of a dare-devil and, if the truth be told, she was a little bit that way herself.

'Reduce height,' he told her, as they flew really low to the ground one sunny morning.

She started a descent and felt as if she might clip the tree tops.

'Further,' he ordered.

Taking a deep breath, Betty went even closer to the ground. It was scary, but it was thrilling too.

'Here,' he said, after she'd finished her lesson. 'Let me show you how this aircraft can fly.'

They were in a 420 horsepower Vultee BT-15, which was known for its low flying. Taking over the controls, the instructor proceeded to dive right in the direction of a group of his friends who were having a barbecue. Three times he dived at them and then turned the aircraft round at what seemed like the very last minute. He thought it was very funny, which is probably why he was given a different job and no longer allowed to instruct trainee pilots. There's fun and there's stupidity; his showing off was just plain stupid.

Ever since her conversation with Mrs Bowman years before, Betty's heart was set on serving God by doing some kind of missionary work that involved flying. Nothing like that existed and she couldn't see how it would work, but her heart and mind were fixed.

* * *

One day a letter arrived at the base for Betty.

'That looks interesting,' her friend said, noticing that Betty had read her mail three times.

'Yes, it is,' she replied. 'There's a Christian magazine called *HIS* and the letter is inviting me to write an article for it.'

'An article about flying?' queried her friend.

'No, not exactly. What they want is an article about what I hope to do when the war is over and I'm no longer flying with the WASP.'

Her friend smiled. 'Well, that should be easy for you. You're forever telling us that you want to be a missionary and a pilot.'

Betty's group of recruits was better than their commanding officer had predicted. He said that only one in three of them would pass their exams and graduate. In fact, more than half of them did. Betty was among them.

Having finished their training Betty Greene and two others, Ann and Carol, were given their orders.

'Report to Camp Davis in North Carolina,' they were told. 'You're going to be working with the Tow Target Squadron there.'

What the three young women didn't know when they were given their orders was that they were being sent there to take the place of three others who had been killed in accidents.

Seriously Scary

Everything felt new and different at Camp Davis and there was no time to settle down. On arrival Betty, Carol and Ann were only given half an hour before they had to report for their first briefing. Half an hour doesn't sound very long, but sometimes, just sometimes, amazing things can happen within thirty minutes.

As Betty put her clothes into a locker, she glanced out the window and saw two young men passing by.

'Are you OK?' Carol asked, seeing the expression on her friend's face.

Instead of answering Betty ran out the door leaving it wide open behind her. Carol and Ann looked at each other and wondered what was wrong. They followed her out and found her in the arms of one of the young men! Both were grinning like cats with cream.

'Carol, Ann, come here,' yelled Betty. 'This is my twin brother Bill. And I've not had time to ask him what he's doing at Camp Davis.'

Bill laughed. 'And as you've hugged the breath out of me I can hardly tell you anyhow!'

The little group only had minutes together.

'We're here on an anti-aircraft gunnery course,' he explained. 'What about you?'

Betty laughed. 'We don't know yet for we only arrived quarter of an hour ago and we have our first briefing in fifteen minutes.'

Realising they had no time to talk, the twins arranged to meet that evening. As Betty headed off to report for duty, she felt as if she were walking on air. Even if it was only for a short time, she was thrilled to be in the same place as her twin brother.

A few hours later the pair of them had plenty to talk about.

'Have you discovered what you're going to be doing here?' Bill asked his sister, after they'd talked about family things for a little while.

'Yes,' replied Betty. 'And it's going to be an interesting assignment.'

'Interesting exciting or interesting scary?' her brother wanted to know.

Betty looked at him. 'A bit of both,' she admitted. 'But it's the interesting scary part of it that's playing on my mind.'

'Tell me everything,' encouraged Bill. 'It always helps to talk about things.'

Before saying anything else, Betty thought a quick thank-you to God. There was nobody else in the world who knew her better than her twin brother and nobody else who would understand her mix of excitement and fear, real fear.

'OK,' Betty said, 'I'll start at the beginning. Carol, Ann and I are here to help train men in the military to do various different jobs. For example, radar operators come to Camp Davis to be trained in tracking aircraft and I'll be involved in that. I'll be given a coded route to fly and the trainee radar operators will follow my flight path, record it and then plot it on a graph. Their graph will then be matched to the plotted points on my route and their accuracy checked. The route will be different each time and I'll keep at it until the operators are accurate to a very high degree.'

Bill looked thoughtful. 'That calls for real precision flying,' he said. 'But you're good at that. So that's interesting exciting, am I right?'

His sister nodded.

'Go on,' he said.

'My second job involves night flying. I'll fly over and around the base here to allow men to practise their searchlight techniques. That will train them to search for and recognise enemy aircraft flying under cover of darkness.'

'Interesting exciting?' Bill repeated.

Once again Betty agreed.

'There's more to come, I guess,' her brother suggested, after she had been silent for a few moments.

Taking a deep breath, his sister began to explain her third duty.

'Men come here to be trained in anti-aircraft gunnery,' she said.

'Don't I know it,' Bill agreed. 'That's what I'm doing here, remember.'

She smiled. 'True, and I hope you're good. One of my jobs is to fly over the base dragging a large target on a sheet attached to my aircraft. This will open out as I fly and the anti-aircraft gunners down below will use it for target practice …'

Bill was just beginning to smile, when his sister finished her sentence.

'… using live ammunition.'

There was a silence before Bill nodded his head. 'Scary exciting,' he said. 'Exciting and very scary.'

Betty straightened her back. 'So, that's what I'm going to be doing. And if I ever fly as target for you, twin brother, I hope you can shoot straight.'

'I'll be praying for you, Sis,' Bill told her.

And she knew that he really, really meant it.

That night, as the three newcomers to Camp Davis were getting ready for bed, Betty read her Bible and prayed. She had done that every day for years and was glad that her twin brother did the same. She prayed for him and he prayed for her.

After the light was out Carol, Ann and Betty continued to talk.

'This is some assignment,' Ann said. 'When I volunteered to fly aircraft, I didn't know I was volunteering to be a target on wings.'

Carol agreed. 'But I suppose when we signed up for the WASP we signed up for whatever flying was needed. Don't you agree, Betty?'

Their friend was on the point of falling asleep. As she turned over, the pair of them could just hear her saying, 'It's interesting exciting and interesting scary.'

Ann and Carol agreed and then they, too, curled up and tried to get some sleep before whatever tomorrow would bring. All three were both excited and scared and all three were also so exhausted that they slept soundly.

Life was never dull at Sweetwater, but sometimes it was more exciting than it really needed to be.

'Are you alright?' Carol asked when Betty arrived back from an assignment looking pale and a bit shaken.

'Probably,' replied her friend. 'But maybe not.'

'Do you want to talk?' offered Carol, as she made coffee for them both.

Betty cradled her coffee in her hands for a couple of minutes before telling her story.

'I was up in a Lockheed B-34 doing a towing mission,' she said. The target was flying out behind me nicely and the gunners were down below watching me being tracked by radar. We were flying at 1,800 feet (549 metres) and things were going so well that the officer with me pushed his seat back and settled down to sleep.'

'He shouldn't have done that,' commented her friend.

'Oh, he didn't sleep for long,' Betty assured her, the suspicion of a smile appearing on her face. 'I did several runs for the gunners and then I suddenly realised that the gunfire was in front of me and to one side rather than behind. The gunners were shooting at the aircraft rather than the target! I asked the officer to have a look and he was on the radio to ground control before I finished the sentence.

"Tell them to shoot the target, not the aircraft," he yelled into the radio.

Ground control must have moved as fast as he did for the shooting stopped almost immediately. Minutes later it started again, but aiming at the target rather than us.'

'That was a bit close for comfort,' Carol said. 'No wonder you looked pale when you came in.'

'If I hadn't believed that God has everything under his control,' Betty told her friend, 'I think I would have panicked and maybe lost control of the aircraft.'

'I don't think you would have,' suggested Carol. 'You're too much of a professional for that.'

But Betty knew that she had told the truth. There were several times during her posting at Camp Davis when God seemed so close that she felt she could have reached out and touched him. And most of those times were when things were dangerous, very dangerous.

Sometimes, before she went to sleep, Betty lay and thought about the day. As she did that one night, she could see a scene quite clearly in her mind's eye. She was flying a Douglas Dauntless at 10,000 feet (3,048 metres) and being tracked by trainee radar operators. Then, without any warning, puffs of black smoke appeared all around her aircraft. She radioed ground control to find out who was firing at whom and why. Betty was given a new flight path and told to change to it immediately. She did and the live fire no longer followed her.

'There was a target-towing mission right below you,' she was told when she landed. 'And you were right in their firing line, fortunately a good bit higher.'

'Thank you, Lord, for keeping me safe,' Betty prayed. 'Please keep Bill safe too.'

And with that she turned over and fell into a deep and dreamless sleep.

After a time at Camp Davis Betty and Ann were told that they were going to be sent to Wright Field in Ohio. Ten days later they were there.

'I wonder why we've been chosen to go,' Ann wondered.

'You're here because you are two of the best pilots in the business,' one of the officers told her, and he didn't usually pay the WASP compliments.

He was right.

'The first thing that happened when we arrived here at Wright Field,' Betty wrote in a letter, 'was that we were fitted with oxygen masks, really high quality ones that clung to our faces.'

'You'll need these,' they were told, 'because you are going to be taking part in high altitude tests.'

'What will that involve?' asked Ann.

'You'll be flying four-engine B-17s, Boeing Bombers, into the stratosphere. That's right at the very edge of what we think possible.'

The officer didn't need to explain to the two pilots why flying so high was important. Basically, the country whose aircraft could fly highest would always win an air battle as shooting down on enemy aircraft is much easier and more accurate than trying to shoot at aircraft overhead. World War II was raging in Europe and the German Messerschmitt fighters were deadly machines. Betty and Ann were going to be involved in research about how high aircraft could fly safely.

'I wonder what happened to the lieutenant's hand?' said Ann, after she and Betty had met Lieutenant Colonel Randolph Lovelace II, the Director of Aviation Medicine at Wright Field.

'I can tell you that,' answered an officer who overheard the conversation. 'Dr Lovelace was the first person to jump from 40,000 feet (12,192 metres) and to come all the way down with his parachute open. That was a jump of 7.5 miles (12 kilometres)! He lost consciousness in the drop and it looked as if he had died. After nine minutes he was at 22,000 feet (6,706 kilometres) above ground. The pilot of the escort aircraft radioed that he appeared to be lifeless.'

Betty and Carol stopped and looked disbelievingly at the officer.

The man smiled and went on. 'By 8,000 feet (2,438 kilometres), Dr Lovelace had regained consciousness and was seen to be moving. His parachute brought him safely down in a field of wheat. His only real injury was his hand which was frostbitten during his descent when one of his flight gloves slipped off.'

'That's amazing, but it's still a bad injury,' commented Ann.

The officer agreed. 'It will take a very long time to heal, if it ever does.'

Was this the kind of work they were going to be researching? both Betty and Ann wondered as they went back to their billet.

It was.

Oxygen Alert!

Just a day or two after arriving at Wright Field Betty and Ann flew to 35,000 feet (10,668 metres) and stayed at that height for three hours. During that time a number of different experiments were carried out.

'I'm warm enough in my flying suit and thick gloves,' thought Betty. 'But my feet are cold even though I'm wearing regulation fur-lined boots.'

Everyone aboard wore oxygen masks, most of them attached to fixed oxygen bottles. Some men had oxygen bottles strapped to their backs and it was one of them who came with a note to the cockpit.

'Prepare for immediate descent,' the piece of paper read. It was signed by the person in charge of the flight.

Seatbelts were tightened and the descent began.

There seemed to be some kind of emergency but Betty didn't know what was happening. However, she did know how to obey orders and that's exactly what she did. Later, after Betty landed the aircraft safely, she discovered what had happened.

'The lieutenant meant to radio the pilot but accidently called seat 17,' she was told. 'As soon as he realised what he'd done he cut off and tried the pilot again. Then, when he remembered that the person in seat 17 hadn't answered, he called him. There was no response. Worried, the lieutenant went to see what was wrong and discovered an emergency situation. The airman's head had slumped back, his oxygen tube was disconnected and he was deeply unconscious. Whilst you descended the aircraft the emergency team on board worked on the unconscious airman, renewed his oxygen supply and saved his life.'

As she walked over the airfield Betty thanked God for looking after them in the very difficult and dangerous work they were doing.

'I've learned a really serious lesson since I came here,' Betty told a Christian friend at Wright Field.

'What's that?'

'It's about prayer,' she explained. 'I've always prayed before taking off in an aircraft and, of course, when emergencies happen. But since I came here I've learned that I've got to be prayed-up beforehand because there's no time to pray when things go wrong. Take today, for example. I just had to obey orders and trust that God was in control. And he was. He always is.'

Her friend agreed.

* * *

God certainly was in control one day when Betty flew up into the stratosphere to take part in tests of oxygen masks and electric flying suits. To test them as thoroughly as possible the cockpit windows were opened and the temperature went down to minus 56 degrees centigrade. That's very seriously cold!

'Poor guy,' thought Betty, as she watched a young soldier try to load a machine gun at an open window. He struggled to get the ammunition in place but his gloved fingers wouldn't work and the ammunition and the machine gun weren't helping either.

'I don't think that's possible,' she decided. 'At minus 56 the oil will have turned to grease and the gun metal will have shrunk.'

She understood the soldier's frustration when he just had to give up.

Looking round, Betty saw the lieutenant in charge going to everyone in turn checking oxygen supplies. That was a simple thing to do but it could have meant the difference between life and death. It very nearly did. Later Betty described what happened next.

'Just then I glanced at my own oxygen mask and noted that the needle registered zero. I was not getting oxygen! I felt alright but knew I could lose consciousness within thirty seconds. Trying not to breathe, I signalled the lieutenant and he came right over. There was ice blocking my oxygen intake tube!

Still holding my breath we disconnected the tube, he crushed the ice and shook it out, and then I connected it up again.'

One of Betty's instructors gave her good advice that she never forgot.

'Always remember this,' he said. 'No matter how much flying you do, it is always possible to have a new experience, a surprise, something happen that is unexpected. If you keep that in mind, it will save you a lot of trouble.'

Betty did keep that in mind and she always remembered that God was in control. These two things helped to stop her panicking when things went wrong.

For most of their training Ann and Betty were together, but that was to change.

'I'd love to fly fighters,' Betty told her friend. 'Flying at their speed is really exciting. And it's a great feeling flying alone.'

Ann agreed. 'Taking a jet up to 40,000 feet (12,192 metres) is amazing. So I'm very happy to be assigned to the fighter branch.'

'No wonder they want you there,' Betty laughed. 'After all, you were the first woman ever to fly a jet, far less take one to the stratosphere!'

'You'll enjoy being back in the laboratory,' Ann said, as if she were trying to convince her friend.

'I know I will,' agreed Betty. 'But it might not be quite so exciting!'

* * *

In 1944 Betty received a very interesting letter. It took her mind right back to the magazine article she'd written months and months before.

'Dear Miss Greene,' it said, 'I read your article in last year's spring issue of *His* magazine and wanted to tell you that you are not alone. There are several other airmen who share your vision for using aircraft and pilots to spread the gospel to the ends of the earth.'

Betty stopped reading. It was noisy round about her and she needed peace and quiet to read the letter. Somehow she knew that it was really important. Going back to her billet, she sat down on her bed and reopened the letter. When Betty reached the end, she lay down and thought about what she had just read.

'So three men have been meeting for a year to pray about this,' she thought. 'And they think the same as I do that pilots who have been trained in the military could be used to fly missionaries to remote places. They call themselves the Christian Airmen's Missionary Fellowship, or CAMF, for short.'

The letter writer was Jim Truxton and he signed off by asking if he and Betty could meet up in Washington DC. She wrote right back and told him she would try to find a way to get there. But she had no idea how that could happen.

'I'm not the only one who has missionary pilot dreams,' she told a friend later that day. 'This letter's from a navy pilot. He and some others are in the process of setting up the Christian Airmen's Missionary Fellowship.'

Her friend's eyes opened wide. 'That's exactly what you've been talking about! Who is he and what else does he say?'

'His name's Jim Truxton, and he's inviting me to join in the planning process, if that's what God leads me to do when the war is over.'

'So what are you going to do?'

'What do you think? I'm going to write and tell him that I certainly am interested. Meanwhile I'll have to work even harder at my training and learn everything I can. And that's not just to help the Allies win the war!'

'I have an assignment for you,' Betty was told, in July 1944. 'You have to go to the Pentagon to meet an official from the WASP.'

The Pentagon is the *United States Department of Defense* and it is just on the other side of the Potomac River from Washington DC!

Betty smiled. She'd never been sent to the Pentagon before. God's timing was perfect! Of course, because God's timing was perfect, Jim Truxton was able to get to Washington DC when Betty was there and they met at the Shoreham Hotel, where she was staying. They had so much to say to each other!

'Do you think you might be willing to join CAMF?' Jim asked, before he left the hotel.

'I'm very interested,' replied Betty. 'Meanwhile I'll think about it and pray about it.'

A month later another letter came from Jim.

'Would you be prepared to open CAMF's first office in Los Angeles?' she read.

That set Betty thinking about what she should do.

'I don't want to leave the WASP while I'm still being useful,' she thought. 'But God's timing was so perfect getting me to Washington DC, I'm sure his timing will be perfect about this too.'

'I want you to co-pilot a Lockheed C-60 Loadstar flight to Tampa, Florida,' said Colonel Donahue, who worked with Betty in the equipment laboratory.

The pair of them were to transport paratroopers to the Gulf waters where the men would perform jumps into the sea. That flight was one Betty never forgot.

'Look at those views!' she said to Colonel Donahue.

They were flying through a canyon of clouds at 7,500 feet (2,286 metres). It was like being carried on a constantly changing rainbow!

'That's the most beautiful flight I've ever been on,' Betty said, as they closed down the engine in Atlanta.

Colonel Donahue agreed.

* * *

Down the runway they walked, still talking about the flight.

'Have you heard the news?' someone yelled.

Betty looked round. The questioner was wearing the WASP uniform.

'What news is that?' asked Betty.

The young woman looked upset and Betty wondered what terrible thing had happened. Had an aircraft come down? Had some pilots been lost?

'The WASP is being shut down in November or December,' she was told. 'We're losing our jobs!'

There was hardly any time for the two women to talk as Betty had to get back to her aircraft for the flight from Atlanta to Tampa.

The stopover at Tampa was long enough for Betty to think about what she'd heard.

'They promised that the WASP would become part of the Army Air Force,' she thought. 'Now that's not happening. There are going to be 900 women very disappointed and jobless, me included.'

Then the perfect timing of it all came into her mind and Betty smiled, even though she still felt very sorry for all her friends.

'If the WASP is disbanded, then I'm free to go to Los Angeles to open an office for CAMF there,' Betty realised.

And that's how it happened that Betty Greene stopped flying for the WASP in October 1944.

* * *

Six weeks later, after a time at home in lovely countryside with her family, Betty was trying to get used to the idea of living in a city.

'You are welcome to have a room in our home,' said Dawson Trotman, who picked Betty up at the railway station when she arrived in Los Angeles.

'Thanks very much indeed,' Betty replied. 'But I hope it won't be a nuisance having someone to stay long-term.'

Later, thinking back to what she'd said, Betty found herself giggling. Mr Trotman's house turned out to be big enough for forty people without them tripping over each other!

Writing home, she told her parents. 'The Trotmans' home is a two-storey mansion with plenty of rooms in the attic. It has twin turrets and a huge veranda that runs the whole length of the house. It belongs to a Christian organisation and many different people live here along with the Trotman family.'

Then Betty wrote a message to her mum before reaching the end of her letter.

'Mum,' do you remember me saying how much I'd miss the trees at home when I moved to Los Angeles? Well there are magnificent magnolia trees in the garden here and they are beautiful. God is SO good!'

* * *

That night Betty lay on her bed and thought.

'Three months ago the idea of CAMF was a dream, a plan for the future. Now it's all suddenly happening.'

Then she thought back to when she was seventeen years old and to the day she went to talk to her friend Mrs Bowman. What was it the woman had said? Betty remembered Mrs Bowman's words. 'You know, it seems to me that God often makes us love doing things so that we will do them. That's sometimes how he shows us what he wants us to do.'

Betty thought of the years that had passed since then and realised that was exactly what God had done. He had given her a love of flying so that she would learn to fly. He had also given her a love of missions and she was now helping to start up a new mission. Her Heavenly Father was going to use her experience as a pilot and her missionary heart to do the work that he wanted her to do. Had she not been exhausted that night Betty might have tossed and turned because she was so excited. She didn't.

A New Beginning

It was November 1944 and nearly all of the Greene family members were at home.

'Joe and Al are here along with their wives and children,' Mrs Greene wrote to a friend. 'And Betty arrived the other day. The only one who is missing is Bill, and we really do miss him.'

Joe and Al were Betty's older brothers whom she'd not seen for a while. Because of the war the family didn't often all get together.

'Aunt Betty,' said her oldest nephew, 'is it true that you used to fly aircraft to be shot at?'

Laughing aloud, Betty explained that she had flown aircraft with targets behind them and the shooting was meant to be at the targets, though sometimes the gunners got it wrong.

'But you're not going to be doing that any more, are you?' asked her niece. 'Dad said you would tell us all about your new job. Is there time to do that now?'

'I think there is,' agreed her aunt. 'Though there's not really much I can tell you. It's still somewhere between a dream and a plan.'

Her niece smiled. 'I like dreams,' she said.

'And I like planning things,' added her nephew.

The three of them sat in front of a blazing log fire and Betty began to talk to the children. Somehow word spread to the others in the house and, before she'd said more than a sentence or two, the whole family was gathered around to hear what she had to say.

'Lots of bad things happen during wars,' Betty began. 'But some good things happen too. And one of the good things that has happened during this war is that thousands of men have been trained as pilots.'

'And some women,' Joe pointed out.

Betty grinned. 'That's right. And some women and I'm one of them. So when the war ends, and fighter pilots are no longer needed to fight in the war, there will be many men … and women! … who are able to fly but don't have jobs in flying.'

'What will they all do?' asked Mrs Greene. 'There are very few jobs for pilots apart from war work.'

Joe was thinking forward. 'The day will come when people will fly all over the place rather than do long train journeys. For example, I can imagine that flights will go regularly from Seattle to New York several times a week.'

'You have a very good imagination, Son,' said Mr Greene. 'But I don't think you'll live to see the day.'

* * *

The talk about flying went on for a while.

'Do you want to discuss the future of flying or would you like me to tell you about my future?' Betty asked, laughing at her family who had gone away off the point.

'Sure thing, Sis,' said Joe. 'Fly on!'

'Well,' laughed Betty, 'there are some pilots, and I'm one of them, who think that flying could be used in missionary work. For example, using small aircraft we could reach remote parts of faraway countries that nobody has ever gone to by road because there are no roads.'

'But there won't be airports there either,' her nephew pointed out.

'You really do like planning,' his aunt smiled. 'And you're quite right. But small aircraft don't need big airports, they only need landing strips. And some aircraft don't even need landing strips; they can land on water. So, for example, there are many places along the length of the River Amazon that are totally cut off from the rest of the world where amphibious aircraft could land.'

Her nephew, who really did have a mind for planning, asked some very sensible questions.

'Wouldn't you need a headquarters somewhere to organise a flying service?'

'Yes,' Betty replied. 'And we have an office in Los Angeles. I've been to see it and I'm the one who is going to be working there. Mind you,' she laughed, 'it's very much a small office rather than a grand headquarters!'

'Are you the only pilot?' he wanted to know.

'No, there are a few others. But they are still involved in war service. I'm the only one who is free to set up the office.'

'Where will you get aircraft from?' was her nephew's last question.

Betty had no answer. 'We're not at that stage yet,' she explained. 'First I've got to find out if aircraft can be used in missionary service, and what kinds would be most suitable.'

It was Joe's turn to ask a question.

'Do you have a name?' he wanted to know.

'Yes,' Betty said. 'We're the Christian Airmen's Missionary Fellowship.'

'What about airwomen?' her niece asked. 'You are going to be the Christian Airmen's Missionary Fellowship's only worker and you're an airwoman!'

Everyone laughed.

'Let's just shorten it to CAMF and that covers both,' suggested her aunt.

Betty's nephew was not the only good planner in the family. She already had her ideas about what her new job would involve. When she moved into the new CAMF office in Los Angeles she laid a sheet of paper on her desk. On it were the eight aims she had worked out for CAMF. Betty stood by a window and read through each of them.

'One, to help Christian airmen who have worked with the military to find ways of using their flying training after the war is over.'

Betty thought about Jim Truxton and others and prayed that God would guide the right pilots to work with CAMF.

'Two,' she read aloud, 'to provide missionary bases around the world where aircraft, pilots and mechanics could live, bases that wouldn't cost too much money.'

In her mind's eye Betty could picture little CAMF compounds in countries like Mexico, Kenya and India. There were so many places where small aircraft would be a great help.

'Three, to help take missionaries and their supplies to places where ordinary airline companies don't fly.'

She laughed at the thought of large aircraft circling a tiny village in the Amazonian forest.

'They just can't do it,' she said to herself. 'Now, what's number four?'

Picking up her sheet of paper, she moved on.

'CAMF would aim to help gather information on terrain and weather patterns to make flying safer. That's so important,' she thought, remembering back to some very nasty weather situations she had met, and she had only flown where military weather forecasts were available. 'What must it be like to fly in parts of Africa where you have sand clouds as well as rain clouds and dust storms as well as rain storms?' she asked herself. Betty didn't know it then, but she was to discover what that was like for herself one day in the future.

Betty Greene was halfway through her list of eight aims and decided it was time for a coffee.

Now, if there is something that pilots just love, it's a good map. And Betty had a very good map that she laid out on her office floor. Crawling round it, she tried to find areas of the world where CAMF might work one day in the future. Her index finger went from Asia to Africa, from the remote parts of Northern Australia to what is now Papua New Guinea, from Central to South America and to many other places as well.

'It's not just a dream now,' Betty thought. 'It's a vision and I'm not the only one to whom God has given the vision. One day … one day …'

Her coffee was finished.

'Right, let's get back to the next four aims. What's number five?'

Betty read what was on her paper, 'To supply groups of mechanics who could be flown to wherever they were needed when they were needed.'

'That's really important,' she thought. 'The aircraft would be in remote places where there would be no mechanics and certainly no spare parts. So we'd need to train our own men and women.'

That kept her thinking for a while and took her back to the map. She could picture places in Central America that could serve as hubs and from which mechanics could fly to one or two different countries.

'Number six is vital,' Betty thought. 'CAMF would aim to provide aircraft and pilots to help in emergency relief situations.'

She could picture emergencies like earthquakes and floods, like famines and droughts. And because Betty had been thinking about the work CAMF could do, she had taken special notice of the earthquakes that had happened that year. 1944 was only a few days old when the San Juan earthquake hit Argentina, then there were others in Turkey, China and Iran. And just the week before Betty moved to Los Angeles the Tonankai earthquake hit Japan and caused terrible damage.

'Just think how much help small aircraft could be in an earthquake situation,' she thought. 'They could take supplies and medical assistance to places that were totally cut off.'

Moving on, Betty came to the second last aim that she had written down. 'To publish a newsletter keeping people up to date with the work of CAMF.'

'That's absolutely necessary,' she decided. 'That's how people will hear about CAMF and that's what will help them to pray for the work.' Betty also knew that regular news would encourage people to want to give money to the mission's work. 'And aircraft don't come free.'

The final aim was to start CAMF groups in various different countries. She knew that was also important. There was far too great a need for everything to be done from America. And there were pilots in other countries who might want to serve the Lord in the same way.

While Betty Greene was sitting in her office in Los Angeles, the only person working for CAMF – a flying mission with no aircraft – she could see what God might do over the world and down through the years and it was exciting. It was very, very exciting.

The following week a heavy box arrived in her office. No, it wasn't an aircraft, it was a typewriter! Typewriters came before computers and they were used for writing letters. Compared to computers they were slow, very heavy and didn't have spell checks! But typewriters had one advantage over computers, they didn't need electricity to run them.

'I'm sending you this for your office,' said the letter in the box. 'I no longer need it and I'm sure that you do.'

It was from her dad back home near Seattle.

Unpacking the typewriter, Betty wondered if it was one that she had used herself all those years ago when she worked in her father's office before going to university to study flying. Sitting down, she fed a piece of paper into the typewriter and started to tap at the keys. She was a little rusty at first, but before very long she had typed out CAMF's eight aims.

Her next few days were spent typing letters to anyone she thought would be interested in the work of CAMF. Betty's typing speeded up as the week went on and she made fewer and fewer mistakes too.

'I'd like to give you a donation for CAMF,' said a Christian radio presenter, as he handed Betty Greene a cheque for $50.

That was a lot of money at the beginning of 1945.

'God gave us that $50 at exactly the right time,' Betty wrote to a friend later. 'We were able to publish a small booklet about the work of CAMF. It's called *Speed the Light on Wings of the Wind*. That money allowed us to print several thousand copies. Now I'm trying to work out who best to send them to.'

When her friend read the letter she pictured Betty praying about who she should send the booklet to. And what she pictured was exactly what was happening in the CAMF offices in Los Angeles. Betty was praying.

Written Languages

Have you ever wondered how the Bible is translated into new languages? Let me tell you a little about it. Specially trained missionaries (often working with Wycliffe Bible Translators) go to a remote part of the world where a language is spoken that has never been written down. They live with the people long enough to learn the language very well indeed. Then they work out all the sounds that are used in the language and give each sound a written letter. For example, in English and American the sound 'a' is known by the letter 'a' and the sound 'sh' is known by the letters 's' and 'h' together.

When every single sound in the language has a letter the language can be written down for the very first time. Then some of the people who speak that language have to learn to read their own language written down. Alongside that – and all of this takes ages and ages – Bible translators begin the job of translating the Bible into the newly-written language. That's a huge job. The Bible has over 774,000 words in it!

* * *

Now let's go back to Betty Greene. Organisations need people to run them and these people are often called a Board of directors. By the middle of 1945 CAMF had its Board of directors. There was Jim Truxton, who was president, Betty was secretary and treasurer and two others, Grady Parrott and Jim Buyers.

'We get plenty of letters,' Betty told Jim Buyers. 'It takes me all my time to keep up with answering them.'

'And you are often asked to speak to meetings about CAMF too,' Jim said.

'But there's something missing,' they said together.

Both knew what was missing. CAMF had an office. It had a Board of directors but it didn't have an aircraft!

Just at that time Wycliffe Bible Translators were asked if they would go to a very faraway part of the Amazon jungle in Eastern Peru to work with some Indian tribes there. The discussions at Wycliffe might have gone something like this.

'It would be wonderful to do this job because these people have no written language.'

'That's true, but it would take weeks to reach them overland and months to get in supplies.'

'There are no roads for hundreds of miles through the Amazonian rain forests.'

'The only way to get Bible translators into these villages would be by aircraft.'

'I suppose the best thing would be for us to buy an aircraft. Then we could transport translators to wherever they needed to go and keep them supplied while they are there.'

'I know a pilot who might be interested in doing a job like that. His name's Grady Parrott. I'll get in touch with him.'

Of course, when Wycliffe got in touch with Grady Parrot he discovered that Grady had already agreed to work with CAMF. So, instead of Grady going to work for Wycliffe, talks were started about CAMF providing transport for Wycliffe's Bible translating work. It was agreed that someone from CAMF would go to Mexico to meet the man who started Wycliffe Bible Translators. His name was Cameron Townsend and the person who was sent to meet him was Betty.

At that time Wycliffe Bible Translators had another part to its work. It was called *Summer Institute of Linguistics*. These two worked together as one. As *Wycliffe Bible Translators – Summer Institute of Linguistics* is such a long name we will just talk about Wycliffe Bible Translators, or just Wycliffe from now on. It will take you less time to read the book!

'2nd September, 1945,' Betty wrote in her diary. 'World War II has ended!'

That was a wonderful day. Millions of people in many countries all over the world celebrated.

Just a week later Betty and the others at CAMF celebrated as she flew (as a passenger) on a flight from Los Angeles to Mexico City for two weeks of conference there. It was a dramatic journey. Thunder crashed around them and lightning slashed the skies.

'I'm happy to let the pilot fly the aircraft,' thought Betty, as she relaxed in her passenger seat.

'There will be times when we're discussing translation work rather than travel,' Cameron Townsend told Betty. 'I've asked a couple to show you round Mexico City at those times.'

'And I'd like to meet up with a woman who served in the WASP,' said Betty. 'She helps run an airline in Mexico City. I'll try to find out from her about Mexican aviation rules.'

Betty Greene didn't waste any time. Before the end of the conference she passed all the tests and was awarded a Pilot's License for flying in Mexico!

'I've visited Chapultepec Castle,' she wrote to a friend. 'It's built on a hill 2,388 metres (7,638 feet) above sea level and on top of the remains of ancient Aztec buildings. Just before World War II broke out the Mexican president announced that the castle would become a national museum. That took years to organise and it just opened about six months ago. So it's brand sparking new. An amazing place!'

* * *

'Here comes the questioner,' one of the Wycliffe missionaries joked, when Betty appeared alongside him with her large notebook and pen. 'What do you want to ask this time?'

She smiled patiently. 'CAMF will only know if we can help you if we understand all that you do, all the journeys you make or would like to make, along with the distances involved and details of the local terrains.'

The missionary smiled. 'I know, I know,' he said. 'And you'll have pages and pages and pages of answers to study when you get back home at the end of your fortnight here.'

'I'd like to speak to you,' said Cameron Townsend to Betty one afternoon.

They sat down together at a window seat which had a view out to Mexico City.

'Are you in a special hurry to get back to Los Angeles at the end of this conference?' he asked.

Betty thought about it. Yes, there was plenty of work to be done but nothing that needed attention urgently or immediately.

'Would you consider going down to our jungle camp where translators spend the last few months of their training before heading out to different people groups?' asked Mr Townsend. 'That would let you see for yourself what the terrain is like and whether or not you think aircraft would really advance the work.'

* * *

Betty thought and prayed about it before agreeing that would be an excellent thing to do.

'How do we get there?' she asked.

Cameron Townsend smiled. 'Perhaps one day the answer to your question will be by air. For now it involves an overnight journey on a narrow-gauge train that creaks and rumbles its way along. That takes us as far as Vera Cruz where, after a night's rest, we catch another train that chugs south towards the Pacific Ocean. We leave that train at Juchitan on a stop-over visit to some missionaries.'

Betty followed Cameron's words on a mental map of Mexico. Pilots are good with maps and can usually picture them in their heads. Betty certainly could.

'And that's not the end of the journey,' said Cameron. 'There's another train ride and some more visits before you fly to El Real, which is a 460 metre (1,500 feet) long airstrip about 3 miles (5 kilometres) from the jungle training camp.'

The journey took longer than expected, especially as Betty fell ill with malaria on the way. By the time she arrived at the jungle training camp she could see what an amazing difference CAMF could make to the work of the Bible translators.

'I lived with the missionaries there for two months,' she told people afterwards. 'And it really opened my eyes to how these translators live and work. I stayed in a tiny mud hut with another female missionary and our kitchen was a second, even smaller, mud hut. The cooker was a single-burner stove. A family (or maybe it was two families) of rats lived in the wooden beams. One day a cow smashed into the kitchen to visit us and several times we had our laundry, that was hanging out to dry, eaten by wild Mexican donkeys. Mosquitoes were a menace and I wasn't the only one who suffered from malaria.'

'What did you do at the jungle camp?' she was often asked when she went out to speak about CAMF after she returned to Los Angeles.

'The Wycliffe training is very strict,' Betty Greene explained, 'and I had to fit in with it. In fact, it was a bit like being back with the WASP again, only we didn't have cows, mosquitoes and wild burros in Camp Davis. This is how our days panned out. I was up at 6 am, breakfast was at 7 am and then we studied Spanish for two hours. After that we worked in the garden for a couple of hours. And that was no gentle weeding and picking carrots. It was more like breaking rocks and hard labour than a nice relaxing hobby! After lunch there was another hour of Spanish.

We all did different things in the afternoons. Most of my afternoon times were spent studying maps, writing reports and trying to work out how best CAMF could help Wycliffe Bible Translators. I studied different types of aircraft and the terrains that would suit each one of them to assess which aircraft could be used in which places.'

* * *

'What aircraft did you think would be best?' people wanted to know.

'I decided that amphibious craft would be the most suitable as there was more water to land on than flat land. Airstrips need to be built and then kept in good condition. It takes a very short time for termites and other pests to damage an airstrip to the point that it can't be used. There are water hazards too, of course, but they are easier to work round.'

Having left Los Angeles at the beginning of September for a two week long conference, Betty didn't get back to CAMF's office until Christmas Eve. She was away three-and-a-half months, long enough to make her quite certain that there was a place for aircraft in missionary service.

* * *

Just over two weeks later a letter arrived on Betty's desk. It was from Cameron Townsend.

'We would like to invite CAMF to provide aircraft and pilots to help with our work in Peru and Mexico.'

Betty was so pleased and so excited. But there was still something missing, an important something. CAMF had no aircraft!

That night, as she lay in bed before going to sleep, Betty thought back over the years to her visit to Mrs Bowman. 'What would you really like to do?' Mrs Bowman had asked her. 'I'd like to fly aircraft and do mission work,' had been Betty's reply. Then her older friend had said that God often makes us want to do what he wants us to do.

'That's how it is turning out in my life,' thought Betty sleepily. 'God made me want to fly and he made me want to be a missionary. Now it seems that both are going to happen.'

* * *

Betty began to count her blessings, right back to seeing Charles Lindberg flying into Seattle after his solo flight across the Atlantic Ocean. She thanked God for the flights her parents had given her and her twin brother for their sixteenth birthdays, for the WASP and the crack training she had working with them and also for the WASP closing down just exactly on time for her to take up the challenge of opening the first CAMF office in Los Angeles. Now they were reaching the next stage. Wycliffe Bible Translators had asked them to provide aircraft and pilots.

'Well,' thought Betty, 'that's for tomorrow. It's time I went to sleep.'

CAMF's First Aircraft

In the CAMF office Jim Truxton and Grady Parrott were listening to Betty's stories about her time at jungle camp.

'What happened then?' asked Grady.

'We were just finishing our lunch,' Betty told them, 'when there was a terrible bellowing noise. As there was barbed wire round jungle camp we were puzzled what it could be. Several of us ran out to see what was going on. There, in a slightly wooded area near open grassland, was an angry bull pawing and snorting. Then a whole herd of bulls appeared and leaped over the fence. We all headed inside and stayed there till they calmed down and walked quietly away.'

'That's enough of jungle camp,' said Jim, 'though I could sit here all day and listen to your stories. Let's get back to CAMF. Is there anything you learned when you were in Mexico that you've not yet told us?'

Betty thought for a minute. 'No, I don't think so. The only real hazard at El Real is the dog-leg on the airstrip.'

Grady nodded. 'Tell us about that again. It's important.'

'The airstrip at El Real is short, but okay for the size of aircraft we are likely to be flying in. But halfway along it there's a bend. Right on the bend there's a shed that belongs to the man who owns the airstrip. He keeps stuff in it that is waiting to be flown out.

'That's certainly useful for him,' commented Grady, 'but not so good for landing.'

'It's especially difficult because not all aircraft have good visibility for what's on the ground,' Betty went on. 'Take the Waco bi-plane, for example, you just can't see what's coming up at ground level. That means you need to know exactly what hazards there are before the final descent.'

Although CAMF still didn't have an aircraft there was a great deal of work to be done, decisions to be made, hazards to be recorded, ideas to be discussed and much else besides. The biggest step forward was when Wycliffe Bible Translators decided to invite CAMF to work alongside them, doing all the flying they needed done.

In early February 1946 the CAMF Board of Directors heard of an aircraft for sale. In a surprisingly short space of time the aircraft was bought because God moved the hearts of Christians to give the money that was needed. He does amazing things!

'It's a beautiful red 1933 four-seater Waco cabin bi-plane,' Betty wrote home to her mother. 'It has a 220 horsepower Continental engine and it cost $5,000.'

Before she finished her letter, the young woman suddenly realised she'd been so busy organising the buying of the aircraft that she'd forgotten her mum's birthday.

'I'm SO sorry,' she wrote, 'and I hope you had a really lovely birthday.'

Mrs Greene smiled when she read the letter a few days later.

'There is so much happening just now in CAMF, I'm not at all surprised that she forgot.'

Smiling in agreement, Mr Greene said that it was an exciting time for the whole family as well as for the mission.

The first three weeks of February were amazingly busy. The aircraft was checked, repairs made to the radio and a few other things as well. Grady and Betty got to know the aircraft by flying it as much as they could.

'I'd love to take her to Seattle to show Dad and Mum,' said Betty. 'But there just isn't time.'

There wasn't.

On 23rd February, 1946 the Waco bi-plane was ready for take-off and Betty Greene was CAMF's first pilot! As she went through the pre-flight checklist she thought of the 2,100 mile (3,380 kilometre) flight to Mexico

City and then the long flight from there to southern Mexico to Wycliffe jungle camp. Her estimated average speed was 100 miles (161 kilometres) per hour ... which meant a very long number of hours in the air, spread over several days. Betty had two women passengers with her, both from Wycliffe.

'Let's pray,' said Mr Goodner, a Wycliffe Board member, before the aircraft set off. And he prayed for God to keep Betty and her passengers safe and for him to use the Waco bi-plane to do a great deal of good over the years to come.

It was time for take-off. Betty pushed the throttle forward and the aircraft headed along the runway and eased into the air. She circled back over the little group of friends down below, dipped a wing in salute and headed off. CAMF was airborne!

March 1946 was Betty's first full month of service out of El Real. She described in a letter to a friend how busy it had been.

'During twelve days of flying I logged more than thirty-two hours on the Tapachula to Tuxtla run, carrying a total of forty-nine passengers. As a group they were saved FIFTY WEEKS of overland trail travel, not counting travel time needed for delivery of baggage and supplies. My total monthly flying time was close to 100 hours. That's not a lot compared to some types of flying but I also had to cope with all the details – refuelling, looking after the aircraft, making all the arrangements for passengers, delivering messages as well as loading and unloading. It was like being at the gym!'

Some time after that George Wiggins arrived. He was going to take over from Betty as the Waco's pilot to allow her to help to open up a new Wycliffe work in Peru.

The last Monday and Tuesday of March were days to remember.

'We've been called to a medical emergency at El Real Finca,' Betty told George, first thing on Monday morning. 'And that's over and above the flights that are already arranged for the day. 'First we've to pick up a doctor at Las Casas and bring him to El Real.'

That's what they set off to do but they had to turn back because of fog. As they waited for the fog to clear George did practise take-offs and landings.

'The fog's cleared now,' Betty told her co-pilot. 'I'll go for the doctor and then we'll get on with the rest of the day's work.'

It was still only 9 am.

Monday was a very full day dealing with the medical emergency, ferrying missionaries, responding to requests and keeping up with paperwork. Tuesday looked as if it was going to be more of the same.

'I think you should practise more take-offs and landings here,' Betty told George, when they were at the Tuxtla airstrip, 'then you can do the landing in El Real. It's more difficult because of the bend and the shed, as you discovered when you did both your landings there yesterday. So a little more practise before you attempt El Real again would be good.'

Betty was impressed by George's flying. He was doing really well.

'I'm ready,' her co-pilot said, when he'd done some practice runs. 'I had a good look around El Real both times yesterday and I'm sure I'll be okay.'

Both pilots settled in the aircraft, George as pilot and Betty in the co-pilot's seat. She watched as he took off from Tuxtla and did it perfectly. All went well on the short flight to El Real where he prepared for landing just exactly as he had done the previous day, if just a little bit quicker.

Betty felt the touchdown and waited for the pilot to start braking. But George didn't brake quickly enough or hard enough and a few seconds later there was a crash and thud as the wing of the aircraft hit the hut at the bend in the airstrip. The aircraft spun round 180 degrees and stopped with its nose facing the hut.

'Get out quickly!' Betty ordered, reaching across to switch off the engine.

Both pilots knew the danger of fire and evacuated the aircraft immediately. They stood at a safe distance until they were sure there was no likelihood of an explosion or fire. As they stood looking at the aircraft, their minds were all over the place.

'Thank God we weren't hurt,' was their first thought, of course.

And that was quickly followed with, 'the poor, poor aircraft.'

Surveying the damage, Betty could see that both wings on the left of the aircraft were broken. The ends of the propeller on that side had sheared off and there was damage to the landing gear too. Of course, El Real wasn't like an airport today. There were no emergency services, no mechanics, only local people and a passenger who was waiting for them to pick him up. He couldn't believe his eyes when he saw what happened.

Later that day, as Betty and the two men prayed about it and discussed what had taken place, they heard an aircraft engine. Looking up they saw a small aircraft circling overhead and then coming in to land. The pilot had noticed the wreckage on the ground and came down to see if he could help. There was nothing he could do apart from take Betty to the nearest place where she could start the long business of organising repairs. So Betty joined the aircraft's cargo of pigs and headed off leaving the Waco bi-place and her dreams on the airstrip at El Real.

'It's nearly the end of June,' Betty wrote home to her parents, 'and the parts we need for the aircraft have arrived at last. They've taken three months to come. But God is good, Nate Saint is coming in ten days or so to do the repair work on the Waco which means that we should be flying again before long.'

Nate worked every hour he could every day he could and was very grateful for God's day of rest each Sunday. Even then it took him nearly three months to repair the aircraft as thumping into the shed on the airstrip had done even more damage than was thought.

Nate Saint, who was a pilot as well as a mechanic, had the same kind of history as Betty. He had flown with the military during the war and then felt that God was calling him to be a missionary and offered to serve with CAMF. All CAMF's pilots had to look after the routine care of their aircraft. El Real and other places like it really were airstrips, not airports in any modern sense of the word.

While all this was happening, Wycliffe Bible Translators had bought another aircraft. It was a Grumman Duck, a 950 horsepower amphibious aircraft. As amphibious aircraft can land on water, Duck was a very good name for it! The new aircraft was waiting in Lima, Peru to be flown to the Amazon jungle. It was waiting for Betty to come and fly it.

'Wycliffe wants to set up Bible translation bases in the Amazon,' she was told, 'and your flying will be a huge help to the work.'

Betty knew that was true and prepared to head to Peru. As she made her preparations she prayed for the work in southern Mexico.

'Please keep us safe when we are flying,' Betty prayed to God. And as she thought about the accident that had happened at El Real another thought came into her mind. 'Yes, flying into remote airstrips will always have its dangers, but trekking for days and weeks through jungles in unexplored parts of the world, where unknown people-groups live, can be very dangerous too.'

Many things have changed over the years since then. In 1946 CAMF changed its name to Mission Aviation Fellowship, which is usually shortened to MAF. It does the same work today in remote parts of the world as CAMF began to do in the 1940s. But what Betty realised that day is still true. Even in the 21st Century MAF pilots and passengers are safer flying in the air than travelling by land in the countries where they live and work.

Opposition

At last, in July 1946, Betty Greene settled on her seat as a passenger on an aircraft that would take her part of the way to Lima. On a stop-over she met up with a government official. The man looked at her tall slim figure and Betty could see from his eyes that he didn't think she could fly the Grumman Duck. They talked about the aircraft for a while.

'I know a much more skilled pilot,' the official said. 'I'm in touch with men who flew with the military and one of them would be good. He wouldn't cost too much either,' he added. 'I'm sure I could get him to work for $750 a month plus expenses.'

Betty very patiently explained that she was just as skilled and experienced as the pilots he knew – and she didn't mention that she was paid just $50 a month!

In Lima the Grumman Duck was given its official name, *Amauta*, which means '*A wise man in the service of the people.*'

'Do you understand the work you're going to be doing?' Betty was asked. 'The Peruvian government is providing the Duck's fuel and, when needed, you can use air force mechanics to look after the aircraft. In return for that, you may be asked to do flights for the Ministry of Education and the Ministry of Health.'

That all sounded very good to Betty but what followed did not.

'I am totally against a woman flying the Grumman Duck,' the Chief of the Navy Air Mission said over and over again and loudly. 'It's nonsense that Captain Greene is to fly that aircraft over the Andes and the Peruvian rainforest. That's a man's job.'

The following day Betty was introduced to a lieutenant in the Marine Corps.

'Will you come with me on my first flight to show me round the aircraft?' she asked.

'Sorry,' the lieutenant replied. 'Chief says I've not to do that. If you are flying the aircraft, you've just got to get on with it.'

Now try to imagine how very carefully Captain Betty Greene studied the Grumman Duck's instruction manual before ever sitting in the cockpit for the first time.

'What a relief it was to find that the aircraft was easy to fly,' she told a friend when she landed. 'I think *Amauta* and I are going to get along very well indeed.'

Betty never started the engine of an aircraft without praying for God to look after her and her passengers, if she was carrying anyone with her. She knew that however good a pilot is, emergencies can always arise in the air.

On 19th December, 1946 Captain Betty Greene climbed into the Grumman Duck. She had two passengers. One was Cameron Townsend of Wycliffe Bible Translators and he was going to look after the radio for the flight. The other was a missionary on his way to start work with the mission.

'We received a report at 7.30 am that the weather conditions were good for flying over the Andes. By 9.15 we were in the air,' Betty remembered afterwards. 'Thirty minutes later we had climbed up through Lima's almost constant blanket of clouds to 10,000 feet (3,048 metres).'

The adventure had begun.

Climbing slowly, Betty looked out to what appeared to be a sea of white clouds below.

'The Pacific Ocean is to the west and the Andes mountains to the east,' she thought, as she checked her height. 'We're at 12,000 feet (3,658 metres),' she shouted to her passengers. 'It's time to put on your oxygen masks.'

Betty's mask was the same one she had worn on her flights into the stratosphere when she was at Wright Field in Ohio. Many pilots would have flown at 12,000 feet (3,658 metres) without oxygen, but Betty had come across enough problems in the air that she was very careful to do all she could to be safe.

'We're still climbing,' thought Cameron Townsend, who could see the dials in front of Betty. 'And we've a long way up to go yet for the mountains are still higher than we are!'

The cloud had cleared and visibility was good.

Easing the aircraft's nose up Betty continued to climb. Down below she could see the Rimac River Valley and she followed it for (120 kilometres) 75 miles. That's also the route of the trans-Andean highway.

'That's us at 16,000 feet (4,877 metres),' she thought, as she overflew the plateau on the top of a mountain. Looking out of the cockpit window she could actually see the tall grass growing on the mountain top!

Suddenly she was surrounded by cloud and Betty had to descend in order to find a way below the cloud that covered the plateau.

'We're nearly over the ridge,' yelled Mr Townsend, above the roar of the engine. 'It's going well.'

It was. They were nearly over the Andes mountains!

'Radio ahead to San Ramon for permission to land,' Betty shouted to Mr Cameron.

Then, as there was no problem at San Ramon, Betty prepared for the descent. Because of the geography of the land she had to circle round and round and round and round (and several more rounds) to take the aircraft down to the airstrip. There are mountains all round San Ramon which means that landing is like winding your way round a corkscrew. Interesting!

When Captain Betty Greene switched off the engine that day she set a record. She was the very first woman to fly over the High Andes. Maybe that was why the Chief of the Navy Air Mission had been worried.

'We've been grounded by the weather for five days here at San Ramon,' Betty wrote to her parents. 'Now it's Christmas Day and I'm thinking about you all back home. The weather has cleared and we hope to be up and off this morning. The next leg of the journey will take us 200 miles (322 kilometres) north to Pucallpa.'

Later Betty described that flight in her book *Flying High*. Here's what she said.

'As I flew out through the exit corridor of the narrow valley, I tucked up the wheels of the Duck into their retracted position. When I say that, most pilots will think of using a lever or pressing a button and waiting for the little 'bump' when the landing gear is in place and the red light is on. Not so with the Duck. Her wheels were moved up and down by hand. The cockpit wheel, about 38 centimetres (15 inches) in diameter, had to be turned right round fifty-four times. At one point, close to the end and when the wheels were high, I had to take my right hand off the stick, hold it between my knees and use both hands to hoist the wheels into their berths.'

* * *

'You'll be glad of a break from flying,' someone said to Betty, after she'd landed at Pucallpa.

She grinned. 'Not really. In fact, I'm going to take the aircraft to Lake Yarina Cocha this afternoon to prove that she really is a Duck.'

'I guess you're having an afternoon of landings and take-offs from the lake then,' the man said. 'Enjoy it!'

Betty did enjoy it but it was hard work too. She did more than twenty landings on water, each time getting to know the aircraft better.

'I was told that some Ducks bounce forward on landing, almost like a real duck putting its head underwater, but this girl behaved beautifully. She and I are going to get on famously,' Betty told Mr Townsend as they ate their meal that evening. 'I also did two trial runs at tying up the aircraft after landing. I don't want to go to collect her one morning and find that she's broken her moorings and sailed off down the Amazon!'

'I'd like you to do one more take-off and landing and also go through the tying-up procedure so that I can take some photographs,' he said.

When the aircraft was tied up and all the photos were taken Betty announced that she'd had a great Christmas Day.

'What was it like landing on the lake?' Betty was asked by her missionary passenger as they flew the next day from Pucallpa to Atalaya, which was where he was going to work.

'Each landing was easier,' she replied. 'Landing for you will be a little bit more challenging. River landings are always more hazardous as rivers are not straight and you can't see what's underwater or how deep the water is.'

'There's a radio-telegraph operator at Atalaya. I'm sure he'll be able to tell you if there are any special problems.'

Betty hoped that was right and asked Mr Townsend to radio on ahead that they would soon be coming in to land.

'There's the river!' yelled the missionary over the Duck's engine. 'And there's someone standing holding a flag.'

'That's to show you where to tie up,' Mr Townsend said. 'The radio operator said a flagman would be here.'

Betty slowed the engine and lined up with the river ready for a gentle descent. From the pilot's seat she could feel the difference between landing on the still waters of the lake and on the moving waters of the river. She'd get used to that over time, she knew.

'That was a great landing,' thought the man at the riverside, as he waved his flag enthusiastically.

Betty taxied the aircraft to where he was standing and the Duck was soon beached by the riverbank. The flagman had chosen just the right spot. The earth at the riverbank was soft and wouldn't damage the aircraft and it wasn't squelchy mud that might have tried to suck it down.

'Radio that we've landed, please,' Betty told Mr Townsend.

He grinned. 'I'll say that you've landed for *the first time* because there will be hundreds more landings to come.'

That was the day after Christmas, and what a Christmas it had been!

All pilots have a routine they follow on landing, just as car drivers have a routine they follow when they stop the car and get out. Part of Betty's landing routine was to be quiet for a few minutes and then thank God for bringing them safely to where they were going.

From then until the end of January Betty flew the Grumman Duck twenty-three times, and that was despite there being some days when the weather prevented flying altogether. At the end of January 1947 the Duck was in the air again for the long flight back over the Andes to Lima. Mr Townsend was the only passenger this time and he took charge of the radio once again.

'A celebration has been organised to thank the Peruvian Air Force for their support,' he told Betty, as they were flying down towards Lima.

It turned out to be another celebration too. The Peruvian Air Force decided to celebrate Captain

Betty Greene being the first woman pilot ever to fly over the Andes and to fly in the rainforest! It didn't matter to Betty that she was being celebrated. What did matter was that she was recognised as fit to fly in such challenging and sometimes dangerous conditions. Remember, it was in Lima that the Chief of the Navy Air Mission had wanted to find another pilot to take over from her because she was a woman!

That night Betty thought back over the month of December. So many things could have gone wrong, she knew, but God had shown himself to be completely in control. Betty knew that she was only in charge of an aircraft. It is God who rules the whole universe and nothing ever takes him by surprise.

Coffee Talk

'Tell me about your work, please,' a fellow pilot asked Betty.

He was Captain John Little and he was spending several days in Lima. She was in Lima to collect the Grumman Duck which had been having repair work done. Betty loved talking about what she did and it didn't take her more than a minute to get up and running with her story.

'OK,' she said. 'First of all I'll tell you why I'm here and then I'll tell you what I do.'

The other pilot poured himself a coffee and relaxed in his chair.

'There are many people groups in the world whose languages have never been written down. Of course, as the folk can't read, that's not really a problem to them just now. But as transport opens up their communities to people coming and going they are in danger of being exploited. Some villagers have already lost their ancestral lands to wicked developers who have drawn up papers of sale that the villagers couldn't read.'

'I can understand that,' her friend said. 'But what I don't understand is why a Christian organisation like Wycliffe Bible Translators is involved. Surely the people groups have their own religions. And we haven't any right to tell them to change to our religion. Is taking away their beliefs not just as bad as stealing their lands?'

Betty smiled as she realised that this was going to be a long talk.

'If you had the best news in the world, would you want to share it with other people?' she asked.

'Of course,' the man laughed. 'Who wouldn't?'

Relaxed in the Captains' lounge Betty explained that the worst news in the world is that every single person is a sinner and that nobody, not even the best of people, is good enough to go to heaven when they die. Then she told him that the best news in the world is that Jesus, God's Son, took the punishment for sin when he died on the cross and that absolutely everyone who trusts in him will go to heaven when they die.

Captain Little looked thoughtful.

'So you spend your life in parts of the world where languages have never been written down, where people have never learned to read and where nobody has ever heard of Jesus,' he said. 'Of course, giving a people group a written language and teaching them to read and write opens up the whole world of education too. In fact, it just opens up the world.'

'That's exactly right,' agreed Betty. 'But the job involves some other things too.'

'Like what?' she was asked.

'I do some flying for the Peruvian government from time to time,' Betty told him. 'They supply the fuel we use for the Duck and I fly for them in return for that.'

'Speaking of the Duck,' smiled Captain Little. 'How did her hull get punctured?'

Betty shook her head.

'I think you should fill up your coffee mug again for that's a long story. But it's an interesting story and a good example of some of the other work I do.'

Both pilots refilled their mugs and took them outside. It was hot and sweaty in Lima but, as they were used to flying in rainforests, that was no problem.

'Fire away,' invited Captain Little.

And Betty did.

'About two months ago I had a telegram from Atalaya in the rainforest saying that one of the missionaries was dangerously ill.'

'I know where Atalaya is,' said Captain Little. 'It's weeks away from a hospital by jungle track.'

'She would never have survived the trek. Her only hope was evacuation by air. Taking someone with me to help beach the Duck, we headed off. It was March and the weather that day was okay for flying. There was low cloud but we soon cut through it. Things looked very different from 16,500 feet (5,029 metres) for there was snow on the mountain tops all around us.'

'Did you stop off at San Ramon?' asked her companion.

Betty nodded. 'We landed in good time to refuel and set off again but the weather closed in and we were grounded at San Ramon. Next day we were off first thing and reached Atalaya with no problems. As usual the flagman was at the riverside waiting to guide me in.'

'You need a flagman for a river landing,' Captain Little commented. 'The amount of water that can surge down these rivers in a few hours can completely change the riverbed.'

Betty nodded. 'That's just what happened. The descent was quite normal and we landed fine. But, as I taxied the Duck toward the flagman her hull hit a submerged gravel bar. It took quite a while to ease the aircraft off the gravel and take her downriver where the channel was a bit deeper.'

John Little was a good listener. He didn't ask too many questions, rather waited until Betty had a couple of sips of coffee and went on with her story.

'While the sick missionary was being loaded into the hold and made as comfortable as possible I tried to inspect the aircraft but couldn't see the damaged area.

However, I decided that as long as we could take off there was no immediate problem as I would be coming down on a landing strip, not in water.'

Her companion agreed. 'Good thinking,' he said.

'The man who flew out with me was a great help in pushing the Duck offshore for she was heavy with water. Then he climbed into the cockpit and I started the engine and took her quite a long way down river to where I found a good place to take off. I speeded up and watched as the spray was thrown up behind us. Then I notched the speed up again but the Duck just wouldn't leave the water. I had to slow down sharpish as we were coming towards a bend in the river.'

'What did you do?' asked her friend.

'I'd no choice by then. I rolled down the landing gear and drove the Duck out of the water on wheels and on to a shingle beach. I can tell you, I was thanking God for that beach.'

'I'm sure you were,' smiled Captain Little. 'Did your missionary die?'

Betty smiled. 'Be patient,' she said. 'We're a long way from the end of the story.'

Her friend pretended to sigh but he was actually fascinated by what he was hearing.

'Because the Duck was on her wheels we could see that there was a hole in the metal hull. It was small enough that there was really just a trickle of water coming out of it. But I knew from the weight of the aircraft that there was a lot of water still to come and we were fighting against time for someone's life. Then it occurred to me that the beach might be long enough to use as a one-off airstrip. I paced it out and it was! But it was covered with boulders and rocks. Leaving our patient in the hold, my travelling companion and I set about hauling the boulders away to clear the strip.'

'You're kidding!' was the only response.

'Just then we heard the phut phut of a small boat and a pastor and two other men we knew from Atalaya came round the bend in the river!'

"Are you OK?' the pastor yelled. 'We heard the engine rev for take-off and then there was silence. We came to find out what had happened."

'I explained the problem and the three men jumped out their boat and began helping us to move rocks and boulders from the beach. We did it in less than half the time with their help. Of course, all the while we were working on that the water was trickling out of the Duck's hull and lightening the weight we had to get off the ground.'

'I was thinking that,' said her friend.

'We prayed before take-off,' Betty told him. 'We always do.'

'Did the Duck get off the ground?' Captain Little asked.

'Like a duck,' laughed Betty. 'And an hour and twenty minutes later we were in Pucallpa. The hospital staff knew that we were on our way and they were ready and waiting for us on landing. The following day we collected the patient from the hospital and flew her on to San Ramon.'

'Nothing dramatic that time round?' asked Captain Little.

'Nothing at all, thankfully,' said Betty, smiling at him, 'apart from the weather closing in at San Ramon and it taking another two days before we could pack her up in her bed in the hold and fly on to Lima for the treatment she needed.'

'Did your patient survive?' her companion wanted to know.

'Yes,' Betty told him. 'God was very good to her and she recovered well. In fact, God was amazingly good to all of us, even giving us a shingle runway and sending some workers by boat to help us clear it for take-off!'

Captain Little looked very thoughtful.

'Do you really believe that God is able to do things like that?' he asked. 'Are things happening like that not just coincidences?'

Betty looked at him.

'You are a clever man,' she said, 'and I want to ask you to use your brain to answer a really important question.'

'What's that?'

Betty looked him in the eye.

'Does it not take more faith to believe that the pastor and his friends just happened to be listening for the aircraft's engine, just happened to have a boat there and just happened to find us a good way along the river than to believe that God is alive and totally and completely in control.'

Captain Little looked serious.

'Betty, I really will think about what you've said. I really will.'

Then he laughed aloud.

'Being a missionary must be as catching as chicken pox,' he told her.

'What do you mean?' Betty Greene asked.

'Well, with flying all these missionaries to and fro over the rainforest you've become a missionary yourself.'

It was Betty's turn to laugh.

'You've got it wrong. Mission Aviation Fellowship pilots are not just pilots they are missionaries too. We are missionaries helping other missionaries.'

'And God helps you all,' said her friend.

One reason why Betty enjoyed flying to Atalaya was that there was a very special little girl there and she enjoyed seeing her. Years later, when Betty Greene wrote her story in a book, she told the little girl's story.

'Sylvester and Mattie Dirks had a child,' she wrote. 'The baby girl was not their own but was one of a pair of twins born to a couple at Atalaya. Twins were thought to bring bad luck, something that many people groups all over the world have at one time believed. Both children were about to be thrown into the river when Sylvester spoke to the father. He persuaded the father to keep the boy and give them the girl.'

And Betty finished that story by saying that what Sylvester and Mattie did that day in rescuing the tiny newborn twin really made a difference to how the people in the village thought about the missionaries.

Some time after that Betty Greene and a co-pilot were asked to fly a Peruvian government official to San Pablo, near the Brazilian border. They discovered that the President of Peru was going to San Pablo at the same time.

'We're invited to join the President's party,' Betty was told, much to her surprise.

How much more surprised she was when she was honoured for the work she had done. During the ceremony Betty was presented with two colourful McCaw parrots!

It must have been a tradition in Peru to give live creatures as thank-you gifts. Over her time working there Betty was given the parrots, a baby tiger, a turtle, two baby monkeys and a boa constrictor. As the pilot was running a mission flying service rather than a zoo, she had to pass on the gifts to other people. However, she was able to keep a stuffed alligator!

Peru became Betty's home for a time. There she set up a base for Wycliffe Bible Translators, much like the one she had set up in Mexico.

Halfway Round the World

A letter arrived in Peru for Betty in July 1947, one that set her thinking and praying. It was from her parents, who were needing some help.

'Lord, show me what to do,' Betty prayed. 'Is it time for me to leave Peru, to leave flying for a while and go and help Dad and Mum?'

Decisions like that are not made quickly, but a decision had to be made. Yes, she believed it was time for her to stop flying and go home, at least for as long as she was needed. And for the next three-and-a-half years Betty had a break from serving missionaries and a time of serving at home.

Right at the end of 1950 Grady Parrott held some discussions with Betty.

'You know that MAF is now working in Nigeria, don't you?' he asked.

His friend and colleague nodded. Although she'd been looking after her parents she had kept up to date with what was going on in MAF and with Wycliffe Bible Translators.

'Jim set that up,' she said. 'I imagine it will be very different flying conditions from Central America.'

'That's what I want to speak to you about,' Grady told her.

'MAF's first pilot in Nigeria has been there with his wife since 1946 and they really need to come home for a while. The Board want me to ask if you would be prepared to go out to Nigeria and take over from them for two years.'

Betty was taken aback by the proposal.

'Lord, I am willing to serve you there, if that's where you want me to go,' she prayed.

Believing that it was right, she agreed to go to Nigeria. Betty landed there, as a passenger, in the early hours of 18th February, 1951. Looking up at the starry sky she felt she had come home even though she'd never been in the continent of Africa before.

'Have you had a good journey?' she was asked on arrival.

'Yes,' replied Betty, 'but long.'

Since leaving home in Seattle she'd flown 3,000 miles (4,828 kilometres) to New York, the same again to London, where she met the U.K. MAF team. From London to Rome was another 1,000 miles (1,609 kilometres) and then the Rome to Kano flight was twice that again. That was 9,000 miles (14,484 kilometres) in all. Quite a journey!

Captain Betty Greene's work was to be with the Sudan Interior Mission (SIM) and her flying was out of Kano, in north central Nigeria. SIM didn't only work in Sudan but in various other African countries too.

Betty wrote to a friend to let her know that she had arrived safely.

'The day after I arrived,' she wrote, 'the pilot, from whom I'm taking over, flew me south to Lagos, the capital city, to meet officials and get my Pilot's License. He let me fly as we headed south. On the way back we stopped at Jos, located on a 1,200 metre (4,000 feet) high plateau in the centre of the country. ... As we flew we often saw camel trains below us crossing desert lands. They made me think how strange it was to be flying in a 20th century aircraft while they were travelling just as people did when Jesus was on earth 2,000 years ago.'

Another MAF pilot flew out of Kano. He was John Clay and, when a new Cessna aircraft was brought into service, he suggested that Betty should be its pilot. It was a low maintenance aircraft and she wasn't a trained mechanic. In return, she agreed to look after the MAF accounts.

'John nearly fell over with delight when I offered to do that,' she told a friend. No wonder!

When the Cessna was still very new and shiny it nearly came to a watery end. Betty flew from Kano to Sokoto. Her passenger was a mum-to-be whose baby was due to arrive and they were heading for the SIM hospital at Jos.

'There's a storm coming in,' she said to her passenger. 'I'll refuel and then we'll be ready to leave as soon as the storm is over.'

'May I tie the aircraft down here?' Betty asked the airport attendant.

The young man looked at the storm clouds. 'Are you worried about the wind and rain?' he asked.

She shook her head. 'No, I'm worried about the aircraft. May I tie her down?'

'I'll look after her,' the man said. 'Here we use concrete blocks to stabilise aircraft in storms.'

Assuming that he knew Nigerian storms better than she did, Betty secured the aircraft as best she could and left him to deal with his concrete blocks.

Early that evening the wind rose. The trees outside her window were blown nearly double.

'Are you thinking about the aircraft,' the missionary with whom she was staying asked.

'I am,' Betty admitted.

Seeing her serious expression, her host said that he and his wife would take her to the airport right away. Sand blowing in the wind became so thick on the windscreen that her driver had to stop to clear it. Then the rain came on and fell in sheets. The missionary's wife, who was in the rear seat, prayed all the way to the airport. Driving conditions were atrocious.

'There can't possibly be anyone taking off or landing in this weather,' he said, 'so I'll drive right on to the runway.'

Visibility was so poor that they had to rely on Betty's splendid sense of direction to find the Cessna.

'There she is!' she yelled. 'And look at her!'

Forty-five kilogram (100 pound) concrete weights had been tied to the aircraft's wings to hold her down. They were dangling in the air like hanging baskets of flowers! And each time a gust hit the Cessna her wheels rose off the ground and then dumped down again when the wind subsided.

Betty had been in ferocious weather before, but this was the worst she'd ever seen. Looking at the aircraft, she realised that the best thing would be to raise the tail and so reduce the pressure on the wings. But how could they do that? Suddenly she knew that, if they could get two of these concrete blocks, one on top of the other, underneath the tail and make it secure that would hold it firm. She yelled her thinking to the missionary.

'We passed some blocks as we came on to the runway,' he shouted.

The pair of them left his wife in the car praying for the aircraft while they ran to find the concrete blocks. Running with the wind against them was nothing to hauling the concrete 64 metres (70 yards) to the aircraft. God gave them the strength to drag more blocks over to double the weights holding the wings down. The job was done and the Cessna saved.

The following morning the mum-to-be was flown to Jos and her baby was born.

Betty never again left securing her aircraft to anyone else.

Because SIM served the Lord in a number of different African countries, Betty's flights often crossed borders. One flight that was hard to forget took her from Kano in Nigeria to Niamey in Niger. From Niger she flew south to Diapaga in Burkino Faso and that was only the outward journey!

'I'll do the usual checks,' Betty told the young man who was there to help her.

It was 7 am and the weather was forecast good for flying. Her passengers were a missionary and her tiny four-week-old son. He was going home for the first time to meet his dad and the rest of his family. His mum had been away for two months and she was longing to be home again.

'How do you know where to go?' the passenger asked. 'The landscape looks almost the same in every direction.'

Betty smiled. 'Well,' she said, over the engine noise, 'we're heading northwest to Sokoto to refuel so I set my course by the compass. But I also follow the landmarks below. I know where there are road crossings, villages, dry riverbeds and even some rocks. But my main landmark on the route is the city of Kauro Namoda. When we fly over it we are two-thirds of the way there.'

'We're coming to Kauro Namoda now,' Betty said a while later, but there was no reply from her passenger. Both mother and tiny baby were sound asleep.

As she began their descent Captain Betty noticed a haze in the distance. Could it be a harmattan, a dry north-easterly trade wind that blows from the Sahara Desert in the lowest-sun months? Harmattans pick up fine dust and sand particles and carry them for vast distances, sometimes so thickly that they are blinding. It wasn't the right time of year for a harmattan and Betty decided to check it out.

'It's a good day for flying,' the officer at Sokoto airport told Betty.

Captain Greene wasn't so sure.

'I saw a haze in the distance,' she said 'What about that?'

The African shook his head. 'Nothing to worry about,' he assured her. 'The harmattan season is well over.'

'Are you sure?' she asked.

'Yes, quite sure,' said the official. 'I've lived here all my life. I understand our weather.'

This was a polite way of saying that Betty was a stranger and she didn't understand the weather patterns in Sokoto!

After refuelling and settling both her passengers, Betty took off and began her ascent. The slight haze was still there.

'We head west now,' said Captain Greene. 'And we go over the Ahaggar range in Algeria on our way to Niamey. If we have good visibility, we should see some lovely views.'

But the visibility wasn't good. In fact, it was worsening by the minute. Betty saw sand in the air and it was getting thicker. Then she felt a fierce gust of wind on the side of the aircraft. 'This is a harmattan,' she thought. 'It may be out of season, but I'm sure that's what it is.'

As there was no time to think of words of a prayer, Betty asked God to guide her thinking, and her thinking was along these lines as she worked out the fors and againsts of going on with the journey.

'For – this mum is longing to be home with her new baby and her family is waiting for them.

For – we're nearly halfway there. If I get to the halfway point and see a landmark I recognise on the ground that would seem to show the harmattan is passing.

Against – it's getting worse at the moment. Visibility is down to 3 miles (5 kilometres).

Against – if anything happens to the aircraft, it means many people don't get help when they need it.'

'Dear God, help me to make the right decision,' Betty prayed.

'OK, I'll go to the halfway point and look for a landmark. If I find one, I'll go on.'

* * *

Within ten minutes the harmattan began to ease but then got up again. Captain Greene was just about to doubt her decision when she saw a road.

'I'll follow that,' she decided. 'Roads always go to places and I pray this one is going to Niamey.'

God is SO good. He took Betty over the very gates of the airport at Niamey and, of course, she knew then exactly where she was.

'We'll spend the night here,' she told her passenger, who was just wakening up.

'Oh,' said the young mum, 'could we not just go on home?'

Betty smiled. 'I'm sorry,' she said. 'But you've just slept right through the worst harmattan I've ever flown in.'

If her passenger didn't believe her at the time (though I'm sure she did) she certainly did later for the harmattan blew all night and all of the next two days.

When they were eventually airborne for the last leg of the flight, this time from Niamey to Diapaga, Burkina Faso, both women prayed for a safe home-going. And that's what God gave them. As they approached Diapaga Betty had no problem finding her way to the airport. Her passenger knew her way home!

Betty's work with SIM was different from her work with Wycliffe, though some things were the same.

Courage has Wings

Because SIM ran hospitals and clinics in a number of countries, as well as schools and other services, she had more medical flying, and more tiny babies to take home to their older brothers and sisters.

On the Move Again

Sorry as she was to leave Nigeria, the time came for Betty to return to the United States in December 1952. But although she left Africa, Africa never left her heart. After touring the US telling others about the work of Mission Aviation Fellowship, she was asked to consider going back to the African continent, this time to Sudan. That set her to prayer and God led her to accept the challenge.

As usual Betty studied the country in which she was going to work.

'It's vast!' she told a friend, with whom she was having lunch. 'In fact, it's the biggest country in Africa.' (Since then Sudan has been divided into two different countries.)

'Is it desert land?' her friend Mary enquired.

'Yes and no,' replied Betty, and went on to explain what she meant. 'The Blue Nile flows into Sudan from Ethiopia in the east. The White Nile flows into the country from Uganda in the south and the two meet at Khartoum, the capital city. Every year the Nile floods from November to May. The floods are needed as people depend on the water to prepare the ground for growing crops. So much of the south of Sudan is under water for months each year. Villages are built on the highest available land and, of course, they are cut off each year when the floods come.'

'Does that mean that villagers become islanders for months at a time?' Mary wanted to know.

'You've got the picture,' Betty agreed. 'SIM, with whom I worked in Nigeria, also works in Sudan. For part of the year they can get around the dry country, much of which is desert. But for the rest of the year mission stations are cut off, missionaries are cut off. Life becomes very different and difficult.'

'I can see why an air service would be useful,' said the other woman. 'But I heard that there was a problem with you flying there as there's a law banning female pilots.'

Grinning, Betty Greene assured her friend that God was in control and that she'd been granted special permission by the Sudanese government.

Betty liked speed. Do you remember how sorry she was when they were in the WASP and her friend Ann was chosen to fly jets while she did research in the stratosphere? Just imagine her reaction to being sent from New York to England in April 1956, on her way to Sudan, by the ship *S.S. America*. Most people would have relaxed and enjoyed the voyage; Betty just found it SO slow!

'Do you want a day or two to rest after your journey?' she was asked, on arrival at Malakal.

Betty thought of the long lazy days on the ship and said that she was ready to work right away.

MAF pilot Gordon took his new colleague to meet her aircraft, a de Havilland Rapide, a twin-engined bi-plane.

'I've never been in one of these,' she said, as she scrambled into the cockpit. 'Wow! Its high up here,' she laughed.

'I thought you'd notice the difference,' said Gordon. 'The nose-shaped cockpit sitting high and forward off the wings makes quite a difference to visibility.'

'It must be really helpful being able to carry eight passengers and so much cargo,' Betty observed.

'The joke we make about the Rapide,' Gordon told her, 'is that it needs to be so big to carry its own radio equipment!'

His companion looked for the radio in the usual place and couldn't find it.

'It's so big that it's built in behind the pilot's seat,' said Gordon. 'And it needs a second crew member to handle it.'

Betty observed that all aircraft have their good and bad points. And she thought back to the accident at the jungle camp and realised that no way could you not see a shed from the cockpit of a Rapide.

Ever since she was young Betty had been interested in different people-groups, and that was one of her subjects at university. That's why she was excited when Gordon told her that they would meet some Nuer people when they landed at Nasir.

'Tell me about them,' she said, as they continued on their 120 mile (193 kilometre) flight.

'The people are cattle herders,' Gordon began. 'All their lives revolve around their cattle and that's what they want to talk about and it's virtually all they want to eat ... and drink. You'll find it difficult to believe, but a mix of cow's milk and cow's blood is a really refreshing Nuer drink.'

'Too right I find it difficult to believe,' was the response.

'When a Nuer man wants to marry he has to pay for his wife by giving her parents some of his cattle. Their beasts are like their bank accounts and they look after them very, very well.'

What Gordon didn't think to mention was that the Nuer are tall. Betty was more than a little surprised to find that many of the people she saw at Nasir were over 213 centimetres (7 feet) tall.

On the flight back to Malakal the talk was about work, especially about how to find landmarks in the great plains of Sudan.

'Everywhere looks pretty much like everywhere else,' Betty commented, looking down from the cockpit. 'It's so flat for so far.'

Gordon agreed. 'Most of Sudan is like that. In fact, the only really hilly region is over towards Ethiopia. But you know what it's like from flying in Nigeria, you study the landscape like you study a map and you get to know it with time.'

'I guess there are two completely different landscapes here, one in the dry season and one when the Nile floods.'

'That's exactly right,' the pilot said.

Over the next two months Captain Betty Greene flew the Rapide, usually carrying eight passengers at a time and often having a hold full of a most amazing mixture of things: animal, vegetable and mineral!

On the last day of August that year Betty was in the air once again, this time piloting the Rapide in the direction of the United Kingdom. She was carrying the King family as passengers. Stuart King was one of the founders of MAF in the U.K. He had served in the Royal Air Force and he was an aircraft engineer.

Betty had planned the flight with huge care and this is how it worked out.

Day 1   Khartoum (where it was 42 degrees centrigrade) to Wadi Halfa – 450 miles (724 kilometres) north.

Day 2   Wadi Halfa to Cairo in Egypt with a refuelling stop at Asyut. And from Cairo to Mersa

Matruk, about 150 miles (241 kilometres) from Egypt's border with Libya.

Day 3   From Mersa Matruk to Tripoli with a stop-off at Banina on the Mediterranean Sea.

Day 4   was Sunday and a welcome day of rest.

Day 5   After a late start because of fog Betty took her passengers to Tunis and then Ajaccio on the lovely island of Corsica.

Day 6   Over the chilly Alps, across France and the English Channel to her final landing at Croydon in England.

Writing about that flight later, Betty said, 'The 4,000 miles (6,437 kilometres) from Malakal to Croydon took 38 hours and 50 minutes flying time. We had no problems with the aircraft on the entire flight. Everything went beautifully. The Lord was good to us. We felt the prayers of God's people being answered.'

But why was Betty flying the de Havilland Rapide all the way from Sudan to England? That sturdy aircraft that she had so much enjoyed flying was in England to be sold. Then how would Betty get back to work in Sudan? The answer to that question was packed in wooden crates. Stuart King was about to have the biggest boxes of building blocks that you can imagine. Actually, I don't think you could imagine them at all!

* * *

Mission Aviation Fellowship had bought a Cessna 180 aircraft. It was transported to the U.K., not by a pilot flying it there, but by being taken to bits, packed in crates, sealed down and sent in the hold of another aircraft. Stuart King's massive job was to rebuild it. If you like Lego or Meccano, you can imagine his excitement when he began to open the crates. And, if you really like Lego or Meccano, you can try to imagine what he felt when he discovered that the people who had taken the Cessna to bits had not named or numbered the parts but had just piled everything in together – even the nuts and bolts! A job that should have taken one week ended up taking a month.

'Bringing the Rapide to England was easy compared to taking the Cessna back to Sudan,' Betty said to Stuart, as they looked at a map together.

He and his family were returning with Betty, Stuart as radio operator and the others as passengers.

'As I see it we have two problems,' she said. 'First, the air authorities are objecting to my route because the Cessna is a single-engine aircraft. Second, the Suez War means we can't go back the same way as we came.'

Stuart King agreed. 'We certainly can't go by Egypt. That wouldn't be wise, even if we were given permission, which I doubt we would be.'

That's why the flight diary read as follows and why the route was 8,000 miles (12,875 kilometres) long, almost exactly twice the distance!

Day 1   London Airport to Bordeaux in France via Versailles for refuelling.

Day 2   Bordeaux to Madrid in Spain.

Day 3   Madrid to Tangier in Morocco for fuel and then on to Casablanca.

Day 4   From Casablanca to Cape Juby for fuel and drinking water and from there to Dakhia.

Day 5   From Dakhia to Banjoul in Gambia.

Day 6   From Banjoul over Portuguese Guinea and on to Freetown in Sierra Leone.

I'll leave you to work out the rest with a map if you want to, for that only took them to the halfway point of their journey!

Think about it, if you built an aircraft, would you trust it to take you that distance in sixty hours flying time over fourteen days? Stuart King was a great aircraft engineer and they had no problems at all. And God is a great God. His hand was on the travellers all the time and he kept them safe.

Did Captain Betty Greene decide it was time for a holiday and book two weeks off? No, they arrived on a Thursday and she untied the Cessna for its first flight in Sudan the following Monday at 6.40 am.

'Time for school!' Betty said to the children who were standing beside the aircraft.

'Yes, Captain,' they replied, as they clambered past her.

Two looked quite happy but the others didn't seem as bright.

'It's not easy for them,' Betty thought to herself, as she flew the children to the airstrip nearest their school. 'Because their parents are missionaries in faraway parts of Sudan they have to go away to boarding school and only get home for the holidays. I'm glad I can fly them backwards and forwards. It would be such a shame if they lost time at each end of their holidays travelling on pot-holed roads.'

'Have a good term!' she yelled after them, when they landed and disembarked.

By then all four were smiling and looking forward to seeing their school friends once again.

Betty climbed into the Cessna and closed her eyes.

'Heavenly Father, bless these children away from their dads and mums and bless their parents at home who'll already be missing them. Please take me safely back to base now. For Jesus' sake. Amen.'

Village Clinic

'What plans do you have for tomorrow?' a visitor asked Betty one day.

'Later I'm doing some work for a mission in south-eastern Sudan,' she replied. 'Before that I'm taking a doctor and his wife and children from Nasir to Malakal. Then I'm flying the doctor and two nurses on to a Nuer village. They go there regularly to run clinics for four or five days, sometimes seeing up to 300 patients a day at the clinic. I'll go back for them on Friday.'

'That means they see up to 1,500 different people in less than a week!'

'It doesn't really mean that. Many of the men, women and children who come on the first day have to come back on other days for treatment.'

'I understand,' the visitor said. 'That makes sense.'

As they relaxed together that Sunday afternoon, Betty told her visitor a story about that doctor's Nuer clinic.

'One day an elderly man turned up at the clinic. He was coughing terribly and was as thin as could be.'

'Was he suffering from malnutrition?' asked her friend.

'He had tuberculosis,' Betty replied, 'and the doctor gave him medicine that helped his cough. Every day at the clinic the doctor told those who came for treatment about Jesus and that old man heard about the Lord for the very first time. He came back each day to listen to the doctor's stories and, by the end of the week, he trusted in Jesus and became a Christian.'

'That's amazing!' the visitor said, smiling at the thought.

'Yes, it is amazing,' Betty agreed. 'And each time I take the doctor back to the village for a clinic week that old man is among those who wait for the aircraft to land. I can always pick him out in the crowd by his happy, happy smile.'

'Tell me more about him, please.'

'There's not much more to tell. He's very poor but he's one of the most thankful people I've ever met. Of course, he's thankful to Jesus for being his Saviour, but he's always thankful to the doctor too and to me for flying in to his village.'

'I'm sure he is thankful to the doctor. After all, he gives him pills to help him feel better,' pointed out the visitor.

Betty shook her head. 'His thanks to the doctor is for telling him about Jesus,' she explained. 'It is Jesus who changed his life. The pills only help his cough.'

'That's true,' her friend agreed.

Later, when she was on her own, Betty Greene's mind went back to that elderly Nuer man. 'Every time I meet him he makes me more determined to tell people about Jesus,' she thought. 'He tells everyone he meets that Jesus is the one and only Saviour.'

It was Tuesday, 11th June and a day that would not be forgotten. About ten o'clock in the morning two-year-old Loraine, daughter of missionaries, was playing in the mission compound when she began to cough. She had some friends with her to play for her baby sister was just three days old and their mum was having a rest.

'Would you like some peanuts,' one of Loraine's friends asked.

'Yes, please,' said the little girl, as she took a handful.

They were very sweet and tasty.

'Are you alright?' one of the other mums shouted, when Loraine took a fit of coughing and couldn't seem to stop.

The little girl's face grew redder and redder and her coughing sorer and sorer. Then her mum realised that Loraine was choking and she yelled for help.

This all happened at a mission station and there was a nurse there.

'You'll be okay,' said the nurse as she turned Loraine upside down, held her by the feet and slapped her back.

'Try this,' a friend said, shoving a handful of pepper in the little girl's face to make her sneeze out the peanut.

Nothing helped and things were growing more serious by the minute.

Loraine's dad appeared on the scene. Praying and working things out had to be done together as there was no time to stop and pray first.

'If only I could reach MAF,' he thought.

But that would mean a phone call and the nearest telephone was 30 miles (48 kilometres) away. There were no mobile phones or e-mails in those days.

'I'll go and phone for MAF,' he told his wife, above the noise of the little girl's coughs.

As the only vehicle there was a tractor, that's what he took. Still praying, the missionary headed out into the scrubland. By the time he reached the telephone it was 7 pm.

'We'll get an aircraft in the air as soon as it is light enough,' said Stuart King, who answered the phone, and then he prayed with Loraine's dad.

The following day, as soon as the sun's rays began to appear in the sky, Captain Betty Greene was airborne.

'I picked up Loraine, her dad and a nurse and flew them to Khartoum, 320 miles (515 kilometres) from where they lived,' Betty remembered later. 'The doctors knew we were coming and were ready and waiting to operate on the little girl. There was a chest specialist at the hospital and his expertise helped save Loraine's life – and he was due to leave for London a day or two later.'

Just a few hours after Betty delivered her precious patient to the hospital a haboob hit Khartoum. Now, if you've never heard of a haboob, let me tell you what it is. A haboob is a wall of dust that suddenly appears from what seems like nowhere. It can be from 3 to 17 metres (10 to 50 feet) high and travels up to 25 miles (40 kilometres) an hour. Betty said that the haboob that day was 'like a great boiling wall of dust and sand.'

The wind roared, the power failed, the lights went out even in the hospital operating theatre. But by that time Loraine was though her operation and tucked up safely in bed in a dark, dark ward. You see, although it was still daytime there was so much sand in the air that it turned daylight as dark as night.

Later that night Betty thought back to the conversation she had with Captain John Little in Lima. And she made a mental list of coincidences over that last two days.

There was a nurse there to help Loraine when she swallowed the peanut.

There was a phone, even if it was 30 miles (40 kilometres) away.

There was a tractor available to get her dad to the phone.

The aircraft was free to get there on time.

The specialist chest surgeon had not left for London.

The haboob didn't strike till after Loraine's operation was over.

'Would Captain Little think these were all coincidences?' she wondered. 'Or would he realise that only God could put everything in place just when they were needed to save a little girl's life.'

Captain Betty Greene was a crack pilot. Over the years she had flown 2,239 hours without a single accident or incident. That was until 9th July, 1957.

She was coming in to land at Asosa, with a missionary family on board, when a sudden crosswind caught the side of the Cessna. Working the left rudder and braking at the same time didn't help. As she had slowed down she was scared to hit the throttle in case the aircraft didn't lift and crashed into rocks at the end of the runway.

With nothing else she could do, Betty swung the Cessna round quarter of a circle. That did all that was necessary and the aircraft settled on the ground – but the left wing was damaged and part of the tail wheel broke off. Checking that her passengers were not injured, Betty thanked God for getting them safely down. But the aircraft. The poor aircraft.

As she tried to work out how to get the damage fixed, the Lord brought it to Betty's mind to take off the damaged parts and fly them to Addis Ababa where there were engineers who could mend them.

'There's an Ethiopian Airlines cargo aircraft coming in on its way to Addis Ababa on Thursday,' an official told her. 'I'll check, but it often comes in here with space in the hold.'

Some time later he returned smiling. 'Yes, there will be room in the hold. And the door to the hold is big enough that you'll be able to put in the Cessna's wing.'

Betty was so relieved and very thankful.

That was a really upsetting experience for Captain Betty Greene, partly because she had a perfect flying record until that day. But it was also hard because that was the Cessna 180 that Stuart King had built from a mountain of un-named and un-numbered parts and it felt very special indeed.

'I know my pride was hurt,' she admitted to a missionary friend. 'And that wasn't right. Yes, I'm a good pilot, but it is God who has kept me free of accidents, not me. And when accidents have nearly happened and I've been able to prevent them, God has given me that speed and the skill. He's the One who is totally in control.'

Later that summer Betty was scheduled to pick up a missionary family at Akobo.

'I'm on my way,' she radioed. 'Is everything okay for landing?'

'It's raining but alright so far,' was the reply.

As she neared Akobo the radio began to crackle.

'The rain's pouring down,' she heard, over the static. 'The runway has turned into a swamp. There's no way you could land here now.'

Betty knew that she had to turn round and go back. She couldn't risk damaging the aircraft again by landing against advice.

'That poor family,' she thought, all the way back to Malakal. 'If only we had floats for the Cessna.'

Instead of a short flight, the missionary family had to travel by river at 15 miles (24 kilometres) an hour in torrential rain. They did arrive safely, but they had some really difficult experiences on the way.

Within the year MAF had a second Cessna in Sudan, and this one was fitted with floats!

'I think we should have a launching ceremony,' the leaders of MAF in Sudan decided.

There were talks and plans and decisions and then the great day came.

'The aircraft, complete with floats, was towed on a sledge to the banks of the White Nile,' someone wrote for a newspaper. 'A crowd gathered to watch what was happening. It took about an hour to get the aircraft into the water. The people round about were amazed to see the aircraft floating on the waters of the River Nile among the tall reeds and long grasses.'

Over the next few days Betty, who had flown float-planes since her teenage years in Lake Washington near Seattle, did test take-offs and landings, always with an astonished crowd watching. Her fellow MAF pilot wore a hi-viz lifejacket for the float-plane's trials and the whole scene must have been very colourful in the bright Sudanese sunshine.

Every time they taxied the aircraft through the reeds and grasses to the side of the river there were plenty of willing hands to help tie her up. But Betty always checked the Cessna was secure. She didn't want to come out the next day and find MAF's newest aircraft floating away down the White Nile.

Stuart King wrote to Betty when the new float-plane was launched and here's what he said.

'It is certainly an exciting business, making history.'

It was. The new aircraft opened up the possibility of flood-season landings in places where that had never been possible before.

Time for the Map Again

Two years after flying into Sudan Betty was on the move once again, this time back to the MAF office in the United States. But not for long.

'We need someone to go to Irian Jaya to review the work MAF is doing there,' Betty was told, during a Board meeting. 'Irian Jaya is very different from any other part of the work, and from any other part of the world.'

(At that time Irian Jaya was called Dutch New Guinea.)

It was time to get back to the map. Not surprisingly maps played a big part in MAF's operations. The map was laid out on the table and the Board members gathered around it.

'Here we are,' said Jim, pointing to an island that looked relatively small on the map, but that is actually the second biggest island in the world. The biggest one is Greenland.

Betty studied the map. Irian Jaya, which is shaped rather like a gecko, lay north of Australia.

'We'd like you to go there,' Betty was told. 'To start with we want you to report on the work that's being done, but we would also like you to think about going back after that to fly.'

Looking at the map set Betty thinking.

'It would be more like Mexico and Peru than Africa,' she said. 'Look at the height of the mountains!'

Jim agreed. 'Yes, our pilots there are not too troubled with sand storms.'

'I don't mind missing out on them,' she nodded, thinking back to some scary experiences in Sudan.

The discussion that day was all about Irian Jaya. Betty, who was interested in different people groups, was fascinated.

'I was there in 1952,' Grady Parrot said, 'to take part in the first ever survey of the Dani people in Baliem Valley.'

He pointed to Baliem Valley on the map.

'That's about as remote as you can be in the whole wide world,' commented Betty. 'No wonder MAF works there. Tell me about it.'

Grady sat back on his chair and thought about where to start.

'That part of the country wasn't explored until 1938, when an American expedition went into the interior and discovered the Baliem Valley. There they found the Dani people, about 150,000 of them living completely away from any other people groups. In fact, they didn't know anyone else existed! The Dani lived in stone-age conditions. We did surveys from the air and found more and more isolated people groups, many of them completely cut off from each other.'

'And none of them had even heard the name of Jesus,' pointed out Jim.

Since then it has been discovered that well over 700 different languages are spoken in Irian Jaya, some of them by fewer than 1,000 people.

Betty Greene did do a survey of the work there and then returned as a pilot in 1960. If you can imagine the island being the shape of a gecko facing left, Betty was based right in the middle of the gecko's back, at a place called Sentani.

'What makes flying here unique is that the island is a real weather machine.' Betty wrote home some months later. 'As the prevailing winds blow inland, they gain altitude quickly and clouds build up and produce amazing thunderstorms, and I mean amazing! So every day pilots have to get up and out very early before the cloud build-up begins. If they're not quick enough, there's no choice but to put off flying until the next day, or the next, or the next.'

'Where are you going today?' Betty was asked, as she loaded up her Cessna aircraft.

'Just the circle,' was the reply. 'From here to Bokondini and then on to Kelita, Wolo and back home to Sentani.'

Her companion looked up at the sky. 'You should be alright, if you go now,' he said.

Betty was in the air within quarter of an hour. She landed at each of the airstrips and unloaded and loaded her cargoes and passengers.

The following day dawned darker.

'I'm booked to go to Ilu, but it doesn't look good weather for flying,' she thought at 7.30 am, and again at 8.30 and yet again at 9.30.

But at 10.30 am it looked a bit brighter.

'There are several layers of cloud,' Betty was told, 'but you should be able to work your way between them.'

And that's exactly how it was. From time to time she could see the Idenberg River below. But clouds were building up on the mountains and soon they weren't visible.

'Sentani Contol,' she radioed, and asked about the weather.

'There are low clouds over the valley,' said the MAF missionary wife, who manned the radio.

'Are there any breaks in the cloud?' Captain Betty Greene asked.

'None,' was the crackled reply. 'There are no breaks in the cloud.'

The weather closed in and Betty had no choice but to turn around and weave through the clouds all the way back to Sentani. As she flew, her mind went back to her test pilot days. 'I could have tried an instrument landing today,' she thought. 'I'm trained to do instrument flying, after all. But there are too many hazards here to make that safe.'

Betty trusted in God to look after her in the air and on land, but that didn't allow her to be foolish, or even to take chances.

The next day, very early in the morning, Betty was untying the aircraft in sunshine and with a clear sky above. Her flight was very different from the day before.

'I flew straight to Ilu with the same load as yesterday. In brilliant sunshine I saw the Idenberg River, Lake Archbold and the whole range of mountains. Then I crossed the high ridge above Bokondini and saw the strips at Katabaka and Kaugime. Crossing the ridge near Kaugime, I flew on to Ily.'

Every time Betty flew into Ilu she remembered what Grady Parrott had told her about the airstrip there.

'At the end of the strip there's a deep narrow gorge with a river at the bottom. And the mountain range above Ilu is so high that it can be a tricky landing.'

Betty circled round, looked down to the wind sock to check the wind direction and then descended to land. The aircraft had hardly stopped when it was surrounded by people.

Betty grinned. 'It's not hard to pick out the missionaries,' she thought, 'with their white faces and the fact that they're wearing clothes.'

The local people were dark-skinned and wore very little. In the cargo hold there was a bag of mail for the missionaries. That was always the thing they most looked forward to seeing for it was the only way they could keep in touch with their families. There were no mobile phones and no Internet in those days.

MAF was sometimes asked to help in emergency situations and that's what happened one day in November, 1961. The news came by radio.

'Michael Rockefeller, the son of Governor Nelson Rockefeller of New York, is missing on the South Coast near the Eilanden River.'

Michael, Dr Wassing and two local guides, were part of an expedition and were on a catamaran that capsized. The guides were sent to the shore to get help and the other two men stayed with the upturned catamaran. Going as fast as they could to Agats, the two guides told a government official what had happened and a boat was sent out. But the boat's engine broke down. Meanwhile Michael and Dr Wassing clung to the catamaran but were being washed ever further out to sea by the waters rushing down the Eilanden River.

* * *

Dr Wassing stayed where he was and Michael tried to paddle to the shore on a make-shift raft. Betty and other MAF pilots were called in to help with the search.

Monday

'I'm on my way from Hollandia to the South Coast,' Betty radioed, as she neared the coast.

'Begin searching the sea and coastline between Agats and Pirimapoen,' she was told. 'Over and out.'

Descending to (500 feet) 152 metres, Captain Betty Greene quartered the area and searched until light faded.

Tuesday

'Take Dr Wassing with you and fly out to where the boat capsized,' she was instructed.

The pair of them climbed aboard the Cessna and flew out to sea.

'It's about here,' Dr Wassing said. 'I'm sure it was from here that Michael set off with the raft.'

They searched the sea area and also along the coast.

'Look down there,' said the doctor. 'The local people are searching too.'

Wednesday

Another full day of searching found nothing at all.

Governor Rockefeller and his daughter, who was Michael's twin sister, flew in to be part of the search.

'I can just about imagine what his twin is feeling,' Betty said to Dr Wassing, 'for I'm a twin myself.'

Thursday

'The search with fixed-wing aircraft is being called off,' Betty was informed by radio. 'Only helicopters will continue searching now.'

She knew that was the right decision and turned back for land. A message was waiting for her when she climbed out the cockpit.

'Governor Rockefeller and his daughter want to see you.'

It's not known exactly what he said to the pilot who had searched for his son, but this is what he wrote in a letter shortly afterwards.

'It is only rarely that one is given the opportunity to witness such devoted work as that which you are doing.'

In the days that followed, many people heard about MAF for the first time through the newspaper reports of the sad loss of Michael Rockefeller and the search to find him. One headline read, 'Girl flier aids Rockefeller.' Another said, 'Betty Greene's long hours at the controls: The woman pilot who hunts for Rockefeller.'

The young man's body was never found.

Of course, most of Betty's flying was to help missionaries in their work, to support remote churches and to care for people in need of emergency evacuation.

Bill and Grace Cutts worked among the Moni people at Homejo, above the Kemabu River.

'Where is that?' wondered Betty, when she first heard of them.

Homejo was about a third of the way from the coast to the Baliem Valley. And that really, really is really, really remote. Above Homejo is the highest mountain in the island, so high that it has snow on it all year round.

As the language of the Moni people was unwritten when Bill and Grace went to Homejo in 1950, they had to learn it from scratch. That's not easy!

'Do you run a nursery?' asked Betty, the first time she met Bill and Grace.

'In a way I do,' laughed Grace. 'But I didn't apply for the job. Let me tell you how it happened. Some time ago a Moni mother died when her baby was born. The tradition here was to let newborn babies die whose mothers had died. So this tiny baby girl was just abandoned. By then we had enough language to ask if we could look after the baby, and the people agreed that we could. She became the first little member of our family.'

'And the others?' Betty wanted to know, as there were two other children there as well as little white ones who were obviously the missionaries' own.

Grace explained. 'Sadly it's not unusual for mothers to die in childbirth here, for there is no medical help at all. So we've just added to our family the babies who were left.'

'What do the people think about that?' Betty wanted to know.

Grace smiled and picked up the littlest baby.

'I think they now understand that we love them and their babies because God first loved us.'

Betty watched the local people with their missionaries and could see that was so.

A Long Trek

Bill and Grace Cutts moved from Homejo to Hitadipa, a village 25 miles (40 kilometres) along the Dugondoga River. Hitadipa was still in Moni territory, but it was a very long way from anywhere, especially in an emergency.

'Grace very nearly didn't make it,' Betty was told. 'She was severely ill and had to half walk and half be carried the three-day trek to where we were able to airlift her to hospital.

'That means she trekked 35 miles (56 kilometres),' said Betty, 'and had to climb up and over the 2,600 metre (8,500 feet) pass.'

'If missionaries are going to work in such faraway places, we really do need to be able to get to them in emergencies,' her companion said.

And both of them thought of the same scary possibility. You see, the Moni people at Hitadipa could at times be difficult and the family's life was sometimes in danger. However, it was decided that an airstrip should be built. The local people knew that having an aircraft able to land nearby could save their lives and they helped to build the airstrip.

* * *

'You know the rules,' Betty was told. 'We need a pilot to check out the airstrip before the first landing. Dave, Paul and I usually do that,' said Bob, one of the other MAF pilots.

'Could Leona and I do it together?' asked Betty.

The three men looked at each other.

'It's a very long trek,' Bob said, 'and the people along the way might not always be friendly.'

'We realise that,' Leona said.

She was a missionary at Homejo and knew the people well and also spoke their language. Leona also knew Bill and Grace and was aware how much it would mean to them to have an airstrip nearby. After a great deal of discussion it was agreed that Betty and Leona would check out the airstrip and that they would make the trek accompanied by a guide called Dugulugu and eight carriers. The two main carriers were Christians and the other six knew the trek because they came from Hitadipa. Of course, they were especially keen to have an airstrip!

'Right Betty, you need to get into training for the trek,' said Leona.

Captain Betty Greene thought she was quite fit, but she still took the advice she was given.

'I'll do ridge walking and ridge climbing whenever I can,' she agreed, and she set herself a training programme that increased her fitness and stamina bit by bit over the weeks.

Eventually the day of departure drew nearer.

'I'll fly with you to Homejo,' George Boggs, who was also a MAF pilot, told Betty, 'and see you through your first landing there.'

She later described that landing.

'We saw the strip from a long distance away. It sat on a ledge halfway up a ridge. On the approach end there was a sheer drop into a canyon. The strip had a steep incline, which meant that if a pilot was a bit fast on landing there was no danger of an accident – the aircraft would quickly come to a halt. As we did our first circle two missionaries on the ground held out an old white sheet. Looking at it gave us the wind direction. On the second circle we dropped down to the level of the approach, crossed the ravine and rolled right on to the airstrip. We went two-thirds of the way up, turned and taxied back to our friends. It went really well.'

Everything was set for the big trek to Hitadipa.

'The airstrip is ready for inspection,' Betty and Leona were told. 'The carriers left as soon as the sun was up and it's time you two were off.'

The two women climbed into the aircraft with George in the pilot's seat. Their shoulder harnesses and seatbelts were fastened and checked. George went through the take-off drill and then they were away.

'This part of the flight only takes minutes,' thought Leona. 'Pogapa is just 10 miles (16 kilometres) up the valley.'

Betty looked out at the 270 metres (900 feet) long landing strip as they approached and was quite happy not to be in the pilot's seat. The airstrip was on a ridge with cliffs falling off on three sides. There was nobody at the high mission station and no white sheet to show the wind direction. Betty could see George working that out from how the trees were blowing.

'It's 10.30 am,' Leona said, as the two women scrambled out the aircraft at Pogapa, 'and we're off on the trek of a lifetime.'

Dugulugu and the carriers were ready and waiting. George gathered everyone round and asked God to take care of them on the trek.

'We thank you, Heavenly Father, that the work is finished on the new airstrip. We pray that it will be fine and that I'll be able to land there to pick up Leona and Betty when they've checked it all out.'

'See you there!' the women yelled to George as they waved to his aircraft.

Eager to get on with their three-day trek, Betty strode out smartly. The MAF Cessna was not even out of sight when she realised it wasn't going to be anything like as easy as she had thought!

'This is steep going,' she decided, as the line of figures tackled the first mountainside.

There was no point in speaking to each other for they needed their breath. In any case, the roar of the river in the canyon below would have drowned out their words.

* * *

The river had to be crossed and the only way over was a bridge made of twisted vines. Betty had more than a few queasy feelings in her stomach as she watched what was happening.

'Dugulugu made his command post in the tree that anchored our side of the bridge,' she wrote to her brother later. 'Then he sent a carrier over without a load to test the bridge. Next went the carrier who had the food box strapped to his back. The strap holding the box circled his forehead so that he had his hands free to hold on to the vine rails on either side of the bridge. His feet moved along the bundles of vines which formed a base not more than 2 inches (5 centimetres) wide. Between the base and the handrails ran vines which held the bridge together. The other carriers crossed next. Leona showed me how to start and then it was my turn. I made it and she followed me over.'

By 3 pm Betty Greene was very glad of her ridge walking and climbing training. She'd had no idea the trek would be so tough. After a break during which they looked all the way down to Pogapa, they headed off through the forest and came out of it a little way from a village.

'We'll camp here,' Leona decided, and gave the men their instructions.

When the camp was set up for the women, the men headed to the village to stay overnight in the huts there. The Moni people wore no clothes and would have been very cold had they slept at the campsite for it was way high above sea level! Leona and Betty were thankful for their tent and sleeping bags.

'Time to go!' Betty said brightly, when camp was struck and everything packed the next morning.

'There's Pogapa again,' Dugulugu pointed down the mountainside. 'It looks smaller every time we see it for we keep climbing higher and higher.'

Leona stopped. 'I think I hear an engine.'

She was right. Very soon they saw George's aircraft circling overhead. He had come to check they were alright. Betty felt a warm glow inside to know that he cared and then she remembered that God cared more than she could imagine.

By the time they were at the pass through to the other side of the mountain range the group of trekkers were (8,500 feet) 2,600 metres high. That day was spent climbing down rather than up and it was beautiful beyond words. Once again they camped near a village where the men could sleep.

The following day dawned with bright sunshine and they were all up and away very early.

'We have a long day ahead,' Leona warned her friend, 'the longest one yet.'

'See that mountain just this side of the tall pine,' she pointed out, late in the morning, 'Hitadipa is at the bottom of that mountain.'

Betty looked. It was a v...e...r...y   l...o...n...g way down!

Along the trek the string of bearers reached a village and, from their expressions, Leona felt there was something wrong. She went to investigate.

'There is fighting going on up the trail,' she reported back.

The Moni people often fought one another and one village could easily be at war with the next one. While the women prayed the two Christian bearers went on.

'There's trouble ahead,' they told the women, when they returned. 'But we've been promised safe passage.'

Betty looked at her friend as she knew and understood the Moni. After another time of prayer Dugulugu went to the head of the line and led them on, trusting in God to get them safely to Hitadipa.

God did look after them and the people did give them safe passage though they saw some fearful things that day. Betty used what little extra energy she had to sing thanks to her heavenly Father. Looking at her watch as they reached the top of a ridge, she realised it was late afternoon. How much further had they to go? As they looked over the crest of the ridge, they saw Hitadipa below them!

'There's the airstrip!' said Leona, pointing down to the village.

Betty grinned. 'And there are Grace and Bill. They stand out so white among the others. And listen to that!'

The Christians down below them, who were gathered round the airstrip to wait for their coming, saw them and started singing. Betty and Leona, along with those of their companions who trusted in Jesus, joined in with them. And by the time they had reached Hitadipa they were one choir singing praise and thanks to their Father God.

That night the travellers slept well despite aching muscles. The following morning Betty's legs didn't want to move. But move they did for she had work to do.

'I'll join you on the inspection,' Bill told his friend.

The pair of them walked every bit of the airstrip, stamping on any areas that felt at all soft, and crouching down to check that any stones were just on the surface and didn't hide underground hazards. There were boulders at the end of the strip, but where they were was safe so long as pilots knew they were there. It was a long, slow and very thorough job.

'Bill, you've all done tremendous work here,' Betty announced, when they'd finished the inspection. 'All we have to do is make sure that George doesn't touch down too early and land on the boulders.'

Not long afterwards the radio crackled into life.

'The airstrip is great!' Betty told George, and then explained to him where the boulders were. 'You can come in to land!'

What excitement there was that day at Hitadipa!

Bill gathered the people together and spoke to them in their own language. This was Leona's translation of what was said.

'You big men and women who are here, listen to me. You need to follow these instructions. You must sit down away from the landing strip, and you must stay there when the aircraft lands. As I have told you, the aircraft has a sharp propeller you cannot see, and it will cut you to pieces, if you get in its path. Everyone must move back from the strip.'

The people did move back and George brought the aircraft in for its first of many landings at Hitadipa. As soon as it was safely down the Cessna was surrounded by hundreds of people all rejoicing. Some were happy just for sheer excitement. Others were delighted that an aircraft could now come to their help in emergencies. And the Christians were thanking and praising God for all his goodness to them.

That whole day was spent celebrating. And the next day George took Leona back to Homejo the easy way, by air! After that the aircraft, and a second one, was used to bring Bill and Grace's belongings to Hitadipa. They had been in storage since the couple left Homejo. As Betty took off for the last time from the newly commissioned airstrip she knew that it would make a huge difference to the people there.

Home

After eighteen months flying in Irian Jaya Captain Betty Greene returned home to the United States. In that year and a half she had flown 1,543 hours, and that brought her flying up to a grand total of 4,641 hours. Her experiences in Central America, Africa and Irian Jaya made her just the right person for her next MAF job.

'We'd like to use you to help explain the Mission's work to new pilots,' the MAF Board members told Betty, after she settled back down working in the office. 'We have to work out what pilots need to know and you are the best person to tell them.'

'What makes me better than anyone else?' Betty asked.

The Chairman smiled. 'It helps that you've flown so many different aircraft. Then, of course, you've worked in so many different countries. And you've met so many different people groups. That adds up to the kind of experience we're looking for.'

Smiling, Betty agreed that this might indeed be the job for her.

* * *

Some weeks later Betty met with a group of men and women who had volunteered to work for Mission Aviation Fellowship. She told them a little about her life's work and then asked if they had any questions.

A young man stood up.

'Captain Greene,' he said, 'I'm a qualified pilot but MAF wants me to train as a mechanic before they'll accept me to work with them. I know you're not a mechanic. Do you think I really need that training?'

Betty smiled. 'Let me tell you a story. A pilot friend of mine was flying a Cessna 180 that developed a fault. He had the usual list of bookings: a doctor needing to be taken to a remote village for a five-day clinic, building materials to be airlifted to where a school was being built, stuff for digging wells to be taken to a distant desert area where wells were urgently needed, especially as the rains were late and might not come. Then, of course, there was always the possibility of a medical call-out. But the earliest a mechanic could come to see the aircraft was nine days away. Had he been a mechanic he could probably have done the work himself.'

The young man nodded. 'I guess I'll have to be patient and train as a mechanic.'

'Better that than have to be patient while waiting for one to come to where you are stuck in a remote village with a poorly aircraft!' joked Betty. 'Any more questions?'

'Do you miss flying?' someone wanted to know.

Betty shook her head. 'I would probably miss flying, if I weren't still flying. But I am still at it. Last Tuesday I collected an aircraft from the factory and flew it to Fullerton. That's where our aircraft are modified to suit our needs. And on Thursday I flew another aircraft from Fullerton to New Orleans.'

'What will happen to it there?' a young woman asked.

'That's where our aircraft are shipped from. Now, that reminds me of something. Would you like to hear a story about an aircraft being shipped?'

Everyone in the room grinned and said that they would. Betty's stories were always so interesting.

She smiled at the memory and then began her story.

'I once flew a de Havilland Rapide from Sudan to England, where it was to be sold. A Cessna 180 was shipped from the U.S. to London to be built and flown back to Sudan. But ... and she went on to tell them how the people who had taken the Cessna apart for shipping hadn't named or numbered any of the parts, even the nuts and bolts!'

The group listening to her story could hardly believe it.

'Did you manage to build the aircraft?' she was asked.

'Not I,' laughed Betty. 'Remember, I'm not an engineer. But Stuart King, of MAF U.K., did build it, though it took him a month rather than the week we had planned for. And then we flew that little Cessna 180 the long way round to Sudan, a flight of 8,000 miles (12,875 kilometres).'

The pilot who had asked the first question, held up his hand.

'Yes?' queried Betty.

He grinned. 'I can see why we need to be mechanics as well as pilots,' he said. 'And I think I'll like the training for I loved Meccano when I was a boy!'

Betty really enjoyed working with the men and women who volunteered to work for Mission Aviation Fellowship. Another of her jobs for MAF was being its prayer secretary, keeping people up to date with news so that they could pray for the work. Eventually Betty Greene gave up her desk in the MAF office to look after her parents until they died.

'As I look back over the years and realise that from one operation in Mexico in 1946 the Lord expanded the work of MAF to over forty operations in many different countries, I give thanks to him,' she wrote. 'How rewarding it has been to be part of such a wonderful team.'

When Betty was seventy years old odd things began to happen. She would drive to somewhere she knew well but forget how to get home. Or she would begin to do something she did very often and not remember how to finish it.

'I'm losing my memory,' Betty told her doctor, as she explained what was happening to her.

Tests showed that she was developing Alzheimer's disease and it progressed over time. When Betty could no longer look after herself, a MAF friend moved with her into an apartment and cared for her. Members of her church rallied round and made meals. Eventually Betty Greene needed care twenty-four hours a day and God's people lovingly looked after her.

'It's very hard to see Betty like this,' a friend said one day. 'I often think back over her life. She was one of the cleverest people I ever knew, and one of the most courageous.'

His companion agreed. 'Betty was able to find her way through Amazonian jungles, over African deserts and round mountain passes in Irian Jaya. Now she can't find her way around the house.'

But all that passed in April 1997, when Betty Greene was seventy-seven years old. That was God's chosen time for her to die and go home to heaven. Just imagine how wonderful it was for Betty to meet Jesus face to face! She had loved and served him from her teenage years and she's now enjoying being with him in heaven for ever.

Betty Greene:
Timeline

1920	Born in Seattle, Washington.
1924	First Winter Olympic Games.
1926	Gertrude Ederle becomes the first woman to swim across the English Channel.
1928	Penicillin discovered.
1931	Empire State Building completed.
1932	Amelia Earhart becomes the first woman to fly solo across the Atlantic.
1943	Betty receives wings and begins serving with the Women Airforce Service Pilots.
1944	San Juan earthquake, Argentina.
1945	Microwave oven invented. World War II ends.
1946	Betty makes first official MAF flight, transporting two Wycliffe workers from Los Angeles, California to Mexico.
1947	Betty averts disaster by making a dead-stick landing on the Napo River in the Amazon.
1951	Betty begins flying in Nigeria.
1952	Princess Elizabeth becomes Queen aged 25.
1956	Betty starts flying in Sudan.
1957	Betty has an accident with an aircraft due to a crosswind, but lands safely.

1960	Betty moves to Dutch New Guinea (now known as the provinces of Papua and West Papua in Indonesia).
1962	Betty retires from field work to work in MAF headquarters.
1963	First woman in space.
1969	Neil Armstrong becomes the first man on the moon.
1976	Apple computer founded.
1994	Channel Tunnel opens.
1997	Betty dies in Seattle, Washington.

Thinking Further Topics

Wreckage

As a child Betty had a happy family life but that didn't mean that everything always went well. The Greenes' lost their home to a fire when she was eight years old. What did Betty learn from her parents' reaction to the fire? Can we love possessions too much? It would be good to think about our most prized possessions and work out what they really mean to us.

Excitement in the Air

It can be hard knowing what to do when we leave school. Betty found it hard. She went to an older Christian for advice. Would you think of doing that? Often we ask people our own age for advice and they don't have any more experience than we have! Older Christians are God's gifts to young believers. It works the other way round too. Young folk are his gifts to older people, if they allow themselves to be.

Women Airforce Service Pilots

Betty was invited to write an article for a Christian magazine. For that to have happened she must have been well known as a Christian. Are we known as Christians? Or do we keep our faith in Jesus a secret, something private that we keep all to ourselves? The Bible is quite clear that if we believe in Jesus, our faith should be open for all to see. After all, the gospel is the best news in the whole wide world.

Seriously Scary

If we trust in the Lord Jesus, we know that we are safe in his hands for time and for eternity. But life can still be scary. Few people meet the scary situations that Betty met, but we all have our own fears, especially as we grow up and move into the adult world. Jesus was a real human being as well as really being God. He remembers and understands all about growing up. Talk to Jesus about it.

Oxygen Alert!

Betty had no warning that her oxygen supply tube was going to fill with ice. When danger comes upon us we don't usually have any warning of it coming. Betty kept herself prayed-up. She didn't wait until an emergency arose and then pray for help. She kept her prayer-life living and active all the time. That's a real example to everyone, whatever age we are.

A New Beginning

One of the first jobs Betty did for CAMF was to make a list of the mission's aims. She realised that an organisation needs to know where it is going in order to work out how to get there. We are just the same. It's a really good idea to sit down from time to time and work out our aims and then to check that we are going in the right direction. That's true for personal, educational and professional aims.

Written Languages

Betty Greene spent some time at jungle camp getting to know how Wycliffe Bible Translators worked in order to know if the use of aircraft would help. That's called groundwork. It takes time and effort and is often tedious but it is invaluable in the long run. Are there areas in your life where some groundwork would help to sort out your thinking about short-term and long-term possibilities?

CAMF's First Aircraft

Imagine the excitement when CAMF's first plane took off! And then imagine the upset when it crashed not long afterwards. Compare Betty's reaction to the accident in this chapter to her parents' reaction to the fire in chapter one. Do you think she had learned life lessons from her parents? What can we learn from Betty Greene about reacting to what seems like a disaster?

Opposition

There were some senior officials dead against Betty flying over the Andes. Why do you think that was? Was there a touch of jealousy or did they think a woman just couldn't handle the job? When we are opposed it is helpful to work out the real reason for it. And when we feel we want to oppose someone or something it is just as useful to work out why we feel what we feel. The answer may surprise us.

Coffee Talk

When we look around at life it can seem quite chaotic. As Christians we need to remember that God is Sovereign, he is in complete and absolute control. When things seem chaotic and wrong to us, in a way that our minds can't begin to take in God is still in control. Think through the conversation between Betty and Captain Little. How would you answer the questions she asked him?

Halfway Round the World

Before Betty went halfway round the world to fly in Nigeria she spent two years helping her parents. Does that seem a waste of time when she could have been saving lives in Africa? Every job God gives us to do is of the same value for its value is in being obedient to him. When God wanted Betty to look after her parents that was exactly what he was calling her to do. His work is not always 'exciting'.

On the Move Again

Just try to imagine Stuart King faced with thousands of bits of an aircraft packed in boxes without one of them marked what it was! That must have seemed like a totally impossible task. The Bible tells us that with God all things are possible. And for us, with God's help, the impossible often just takes a good bit longer to do than what we thought was possible. Have you discovered that to be true?

Village Clinic

This chapter shows Betty's expertise in coping with the haboob and then her reaction to having her first accident after 2,239 flying hours. She was obviously a splendid pilot but even she had to cope with things going wrong. Did she cope well? What do we do with our frustration when things go wrong, especially things for which we are responsible? What do we do when pride rears its ugly head?

Time for the Map Again

Betty found herself in the newspaper headlines because of the sad sea search for Michael Rockefeller and then she was back to her ordinary work for people living in stone-age conditions. Does God care more about 'important' people than he does about primitive people-groups in faraway places? How should we respond to people from different social and economic backgrounds?

A Long Trek

That was some trek – and all to check out an airstrip in the back of beyond! Should two women have been allowed to make that trek? Was that wise and responsible? Now go back to chapter nine and think about the issue again. There is a difference between being irresponsible and taking all wise precautions? Do we think that through when we start something new that's out of our comfort zone?

Home

It was not very many years between Betty Greene working out the amazing schedule for the 4,000 miles (6,437 kilometres) flight from Sudan to England and for the 8,000 miles 12,875 kilometres) flight back and her being struck by Alzheimer's disease and becoming a frail elderly woman. Think about what happened then. Did her illness make her any less precious to her friends and family? Does Betty still have Alzheimer's disease in heaven?

About the Author

Irene Howat is an award-winning author and a talented artist in Ayrshire, Scotland. She is married to a retired minister and they have a grown-up family. She especially enjoys receiving letters and replies to all of them; check out her new stories at www.story-a-month-club.org.uk.

Lightkeepers
Ten Girls – Complete Box Set
by Irene Howat

This giftbox collection of colourful stories makes a perfect present that will delight young girls of every age. This edition includes *Ten Girls Who Changed the World*, *Ten Girls Who Didn't Give In*, *Ten Girls Who Made a Difference*, *Ten Girls Who Made History*, and *Ten Girls Who Used Their Talents*.

ISBN: 978-1-84550-319-2

• Lilias Trotter •

DARING IN
THE DESERT

Irene Howat

Lilias Trotter: Daring in the Desert
by Irene Howat

'You could become the greatest living painter. Your
paintings would be treasured for ever.' Those were the
words Lilias Trotter heard from John Ruskin, one of the
world's most established art critics. She had to make a
choice between her talent and her calling. Both were
gifts from God. In May 1879, Lilias knew what she
should do. God's work for Lilias was in the desert land
of Algeria. Palm trees and camels replaced lampposts
and horse drawn carriages. The desert was her home,
its people her friends and its Creator her reason for life.

ISBN: 978-1-178191-777-0

Helen Roseveare:
On His Majesty's Service
by Irene Howat

Helen Roseveare qualified as a doctor, packed up her
life in England and set off to be a missionary in the
Belgian Congo. Although living through a rebellion
and being taken captive for several months, Helen's
faith remained strong and she returned to the
renamed 'Zaire' to serve the Lord by working with
people there. Her experiences in Africa have been an
encouragement to many and made her well known
and loved throughout the world.

ISBN: 978-1-84550-259-1

OTHER BOOKS IN THE TRAILBLAZERS SERIES

For a full list of Trailblazers, please see our
website: www.christianfocus.com
All Trailblazers are available as e-books

CHRISTIAN FOCUS PUBLICATIONS

Christian Focus | Christian Heritage | CF4K | Mentor

Christian Focus Publications publishes books for adults and children under its four main imprints: Christian Focus, CF4K, Mentor and Christian Heritage. Our books reflect our conviction that God's Word is reliable and Jesus is the way to know him, and live for ever with him.

Our children's publication list includes a Sunday School curriculum that covers pre-school to early teens, and puzzle and activity books. We also publish personal and family devotional titles, biographies and inspirational stories that children will love.

If you are looking for quality Bible teaching for children then we have an excellent range of Bible stories and age-specific theological books.

From pre-school board books to teenage apologetics, we have it covered!

Find us at our web page:
www.christianfocus.com

CF4•K
Because you're never
too young to know Jesus